"The shift to the next generation of leaders has begun. The mere definition of the word loyalty comes into sharp focus and is radically different than previously defined. Long gone are the ideals of loyalty through thick and thin and those who continue to lead with that assumption will proceed at their own peril. Dov Baron's book "Fiercely Loyal' lays out the essential strategies for companies, corporations and leaders to thrive within our new paradigm. This book is a must read for those chartered to lead!"

~ **Dana Green**
Senior Partner, Morgan Samuels
The leading human capital consulting firm

"Over the years of running the SANG organization I have come to know personally know some of the greatest thought leaders in the world, including Tony Robbins, Stephen Covey, Marshal Goldsmith, Brad Smart, Guy Kawasaki and other greats. I can tell you that Dov Baron is one of the most authentic leaders I have ever known."

"If you want to be at the top of your game in talent acquisition and human resources Dov Baron's book "Fiercely Loyal" is your new bible. Read it and live by it!"

~ **Larry Benet**
Chief Connector of SANG
Author of *Connection Currency*

"The company with the best people wins - every time! But you can't have a great sustaining company without loyal team members who are passionate about your vision, your customers, and the noble cause. Dov's new book helps leaders create "Fiercely Loyal" employees who are engaged, inspired and driven to succeed. This is a great and essential read for any leader looking to take their business to unimaginable heights."

~Keith Krach
CEO and President DocuSign

"Dov Baron's new book Fiercely Loyal is a wake up call for leaders who are challenged by how to attract and hold on to talented people. Dov addresses issues that are talked about far too infrequently, but that are in fact the absolute keys to creating loyalty in employees today. Dov's "Full Monty" straight talk will shake you up, motivate you to change, and give you concrete ways to make loyalty a cornerstone of your organization."

"So many leaders say things like "I want to hire people who will be loyal" - but of course that's not how it works. You earn loyalty from the people you hire by giving them something to be loyal to!"

"This book is going to open a lot of people's eyes!"

~ Joe Calloway
Top Business Author of *Becoming a Category of One*
Keynote speaker and corporate consultant

"Keeping top talent should be a priority for every leader, and in this book Dov Baron explains just how to do that. With his trademark intensity and insight, he teaches the practices you need to attract, engage, keep and lead high performers. He'll challenge your thinking and shake up your game. If you want to get better, read this book."

~ **Mark Sanborn**
Multiple bestselling author of *The Fred Factor* and others.
Leading keynote speaker of customer service and loyalty.

"Fiercely Loyal is an authentic leadership book written by a man who walks the walk. Well researched and packed full of insightful anecdotes and take-aways, Dov Baron has created a powerful handbook for talent management that should be part of every leaders must read list."

~ **Lt Col Rob "Waldo" Waldman**
Author of the New York Times and
Wall Street Journal bestseller: *Never Fly Solo*

"Dov Baron's Fiercely Loyal is full of practical tips for CEOs who want to retain their talent pool of the future −Millennials. This book is a must read for all CEOs and HR professionals!"

~ **Nancy MacKay**, PhD
CEO of MacKay CEO Forums

"Businesses today have been slow in understanding the shift from ME into WE. Yet, Leadership from 2003-2043 embodies the heart of this WE Generation. In this thought provoking and instructional book Fiercely Loyal Dov Baron argues what Leadership looks like in WE Cycle and how to integrate this new style of Leadership into your organization that creates a Fiercely Loyal organization."

~ **Michael R. Drew**
Co-author *Pendulum: How Past Generations Shape our Present and Predict our Future*

"Dov Baron dispels the myth that today's workforce is self-centered and governed by a mentality of entitlement. To the contrary, when extraordinary talent is empowered to move beyond their "job" and, instead, cultivate a career that provides fulfillment, monetary reward AND a strong sense of communal contribution, their collective impact reverberates not only throughout the organization, but across the globe. Fiercely Loyal provides the step-by-step blueprint required to make this happen. Read it."

~ **Steve Olsher**
New York Times bestselling author of *What Is Your WHAT? Discover The ONE Amazing Thing You Were Born To Do*

"Yes! Dov Baron gets it. Finding and keeping top performers isn't about bribing them with more money, it's about inspiring them and helping them grow. This is an invaluable book for small and big business alike."

~ **Dave Crenshaw**
The Myth of Multitasking
Author, speaker, and business coach

"Fiercely Loyal is a road map to becoming a high performing leader in any business or organization, big or small. Dov Baron's book Fiercely Loyal provides a higher consciousness approach to leadership, one that melds authenticity and collaboration with serving for the common good of all."

~ **J V Crum III**, JD, MBA
Best Selling Author and Founder of
Conscious Millionaire Institute.

"Dov Baron strips away distracting management fads on leadership and talent retention. He reveals the basis of genuinely effective corporate leadership: being vulnerable, offering loyalty before expecting it and the power of being human (eg. storytelling). Sensible application of his ideas would transform any working group."

~ **Rupert Phelps**
Director of Family Office Services
Savills Global Real Estate Services

In-Phase Publishing

Vancouver, British Columbia

Published by In-Phase Publishing Inc, Canada and USA.

Fiercely Loyal: How high performing companies develop and retain top talent / Dov Baron.

Printed in Canada

In-Phase Publishing

ISBN 978-1546435211

1. Leadership Development – Handbooks, Manuals, etc.
2. Business Success
3. Human Resources

For information regarding the author and the author's services, please contact Dov Baron International +1 778 379 7517

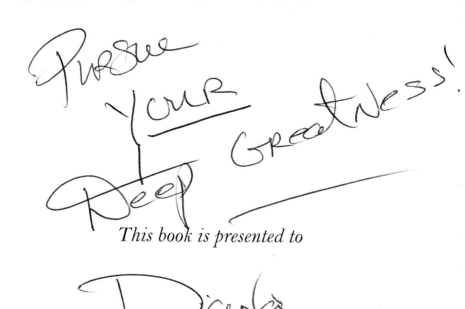

Pursue YOUR Greatness!

Deep

This book is presented to

Diana

From

Dav

Dedication

We all know; life is short, but for most of us it doesn't really hit home until we lose a loved one.

This book is dedicated to the memory of Shishu Pal Sharma. He was a man that I had the honor of connecting with during the last year of his life. Shishu was my wife's favorite uncle.

When she was a child, his home, along with his loving wife Sheila and their three children was a place where the door was always open, and food was always available. This was also a place where as a young girl my wife could always go because Shishu uncle's house was a safe place for her.

Shishu and Sheila moved from Fiji to Canada as a young family. Their hopes and dreams, similar to that of most immigrant families: to create opportunities and better lives for their children.

I believe that immigrant families often work harder (and longer) than native workers because they see everything as an opportunity, while native workers often take those same opportunities for granted.

However, there is a cost to this immigrant work ethic. All too often the children of the ambitious grow up experiencing very little of their parents as two people who guide them and they can laugh with.

One thing I am sure of is this: What we do while we are here echoes in the lives of our children and all we have touched.

As we sat with uncle Shishu at his deathbed and discussed the things that his life had taught him, we spoke about the legacy he would be leaving. Not the legacy of assets or finances, but rather the legacy for his children, grandchildren, family, friends and the community he was part of.

What follows is a summary of his message; I share it with you in hopes that it will resonate with you as you contemplate the value of all your relationships and your commitment to them.

In a world that can seem dark and overwhelming,
many work hard to attain the things they hope
will bring them laughter, light and love.

We may think that by doing all the things we do,
we will be loved. But in order to be loved,
we must first love!

I know that I have worked hard, and at times
I may have been hard. However, at this time,
I've come to realize that it is through the softness of
love shared, that I know the true value of my life.

And so I leave you with this message.

Work is important.
Resentment is a waste.

Ultimately, it is love that is the
jewel in the crown of your life.

It is the love you give and the love you
allow yourself to receive that truly matters!

~ **Shishu Pal Sharma**
1943 - 2014

Acknowledgments

My first thank you is to my beloved bride, life partner, and business partner Renuka: You are my muse, my greatest inspiration. Your unwavering love and support of my life's purpose has been the wind in my sails, and on days where I felt like I had lost my compass you were my rudder. Yes, there have been moments where you have willingly been "the woman behind the man". But that is because when I felt I had nothing left you were behind me, pushing me towards my goals, dreams, and purpose. However, more often than not, you are by my side as my partner, as my equal and I most sincerely thank you.

Thank you to my great friend, a brother, business coach and guide, Alan Lary. You have consistently been the voice that goes ahead of me. You have brought the message of authentic-vulnerable leadership to so many who would never have heard it if it was not for your commitment and dedication, not only to your own growth and leadership development, but also to everyone who crosses your path. You are the walking, talking, living example of the message I've shared. I'm honored to have you, not only on my team, but also by my side as my friend.

My gratitude also goes to my team: Stephan Stavrakis, I'm truly grateful for your constant belief, commitment, assistance and guidance to help me bring my message on the vital importance of authentic, vulnerable leadership to the world. You are not only a brilliant positioning strategist; you are also a good friend that I trust.

Thank you to my dear friend and publicity wizard, Damian Loth, for your consistent belief and commitment, and for always finding new ways to have the world see the value of what we bring to leadership.

Thank you to the entire team at The Authentic Speaker Academy for Leadership: Every student, alumni, and every coach (past and present). Watching you all eat, sleep, live, and breathe the Codes of Conduct and Principles is an inspiration to me. You are all a new bright light on the path of leadership. You are the leaders the world has been waiting for.

Special thanks go to my outstanding editor Woodeene Koenig-Bricker. Thank you for always keeping the integrity of my voice and my message. Thank you for always cleaning up my grammatical mess. I consider it an honor and a pure pleasure to have you on my team.

And appropriately last, but certainly not least, a huge thank you to the person who goes through the book last. Having worked with a number of line editors and proof readers, what I can tell you is that Deb Rondeau is in a class of her own. Thank you Deb for your vigilant eagle eyed skills. I sincerely appreciate you, your outstanding skills and your totally professional attitude. I am delighted to have you on our team.

Fiercely Loyal

*How High Performing Companies
Develop and Retain Top Talent*

By
Dov Baron

List of Chapters

Chapter Sixteen Continued. . .

Chapter Seventeen

Introduction

There's a creeping crisis facing companies today, a crisis that over the next twenty years will affect the bottom line harder than the recession of 2008! The average company spends 1.5 to 2 times the annual salary of an employee training and developing them. The average Millennial employee is only looking at a tenure of 1.2 to 2.4 years, at the outside. That means you will see that expensive employee walk away before your investment ever pays off. What's worse is, the employee you have invested in will take the skills and training that you paid for, and leverage them into a better position with your competitor.

Why is this happening?

In the following pages I will clarify why everything you've been told about leadership over the past thirty years no longer applies. Everything! The world has changed, and so has everything we know about becoming—and remaining—an effective leader when it comes to keeping your Top Millennial Talent.

I've been working with leaders around the world and have had the opportunity to witness these changes first-hand. I've seen what works and, more importantly, I've seen what no longer works.

Successful Leadership Requires Fierce Loyalty

Over and over, I've seen that the single most vital aspect to successful leadership and keeping top talent is developing loyalty from those you work with. Not just loyalty, but FIERCE

1

LOYALTY! The kind of loyalty that means your star players would stand up and fight for your organization because it represents something far greater than a job or even a career to them.

My main intention in writing this book is to help you develop a leadership style that will have your top Millennial talent become Fiercely Loyal. So the question becomes: how do you develop that kind of loyalty?

It is worth noting that very few books in the category of leadership are about developing loyalty by developing other leaders. In fact, most leadership books focus on how leaders can manipulate people into being better followers rather than focusing on the real problem—how to become a great leader who creates more loyal leaders.

In March 2014, Time Magazine published its list of which professions have the most psychopaths, and top of the list was—wait for it—CEOs! To be clear, we are not taking about the movie versions of psychopaths but rather the behaviors and thought processes as explained by the medical profession.

Psycho CEOs
As the article points out: "Psychopathy is a personality disorder that has been variously described as characterized shallow emotions (in particular reduced fear), unusually high stress tolerance, lacking empathy, cold heartedness, lacking guilt, egocentricity, superficial character, manipulative, irresponsibility, impulsivity, and antisocial behavior such as parasitic lifestyle and criminality."

If the list above describes you, then you can close this book and go back to looking in the mirror and telling yourself how wonderful you are, and that everyone else is just some peon pawn in your greater plan for world dominance, because this book is not for you. If you are looking for ways to manipulate those peons (or as I like to call them,"pee-ons")—into being better followers, then once again, this book isn't for you.

I will do my very best to clearly lay out for you to see how the old model of leadership, and with it the role of CEO, has significantly changed. What's more, those changes are only going to increase over time. The role of CEO without doubt offers an environment that is well-suited to a psychopath, and certainly such a person would be drawn to such a role, where their sense and need for power can thrive. That being said, I am sure you know that being a CEO and or a top-tier executive often requires the ability to make objective, clinical decisions in which they must at least try to divorce themselves from their feelings.

However, each of us should note that all of that is only one part of what we do. Great leaders, Authentic Vulnerable Full Monty Leaders, require the ability to develop deep human connection. As you will discover, knowing how to empathetically deal with feelings offers a completely different and significantly more fulfilling power that directly connects with your top talent and makes them Fiercely Loyal. This is, in fact, the direct opposite of the psycho CEO style of yesteryear.

Generating Fierce Loyalty

This book is for those of us who are leaders because we believe we can, and must, make a difference through what we do. This book is for those of us who truly get it that "no man (or women) is an island." Therefore, this book is about how to have your top players become Fiercely Loyal by training them and teaching them how to be authentic, empowered, and empowering leaders by YOU demonstrating that model of leadership for them.

As Richard Branson of Virgin Airlines said so well: "Train people well enough that they can leave you, and treat them so well that they won't want to."

Let's begin by looking at what leadership really is and why loyalty is the single most essential ingredient in every successful organization.

Chapter One

Characteristics of a Notable Leader

What's a leader? You might be tempted to say, "Someone who leads" and while you wouldn't be entirely wrong, you wouldn't be right either because the idea of leadership has changed over the years. What used to be thought of as "leadership" no longer works.

But—and this is a big but—what makes a true leader has and always will remain the same. And when a leader fails to exhibit this one lasting characteristic, his or her leadership is bound to fail.

Notable Leaders

To explain, let's go back and look at a few notable leaders over the centuries. Now I'm not here to judge if they were "good" or "bad." The fact that they had thousands, even millions, who were willing to die for them makes them notable leaders.

One is Alexander the Great. He came to power at age twenty, and by age thirty, he was ruler of an empire that stretched from Greece to Egypt and into present-day Pakistan. Undefeated in battle, he is still considered one of the world's greatest military leaders. His men followed him for years, literally to the ends of the earth, until one day they simply refused to go any further.

Then there was Julius Caesar. He rose to the highest office in Rome and ruled the entire known world until that fateful day in March when his fellow senators and former friends stabbed him to death.

Or take Hitler. You might consider him the embodiment of evil, but there is no denying that he captured the imagination of a nation who blindly and obediently followed his orders, even to the executions of millions and millions of innocents. Where did Hitler end up? Committing suicide while cowering in an underground bunker.

Dead and Disgraced

These men and countless others like them enjoyed enormous power and prestige and were considered great leaders of their time. But ultimately, they failed to keep the loyalty of those under them, and they ended up dead and disgraced.

Why? What made their leadership fall apart?

Part is, of course, that their styles of leadership no longer served. This is true today when authoritarian "I am the boss and I say so" leadership is proving ineffective with the next generation of workers.

CHARACTERISTICS OF A NOTABLE LEADER

Genuine Involvement

But what really doomed those leaders, and what dooms leaders today, is the lack of connection the leader has with his or her followers. All of the leaders I mentioned earlier started out by being genuinely involved and concerned with the people they were leading. (Or at least they did a good enough job of pretending to be concerned that they were able to fool most people.)

Alexander the Great was a man's man, who fought—and drank and whored—alongside his troops. Julius Caesar was at the front lines of battle, inspiring his men to cross the Rubicon and face their foes with his own courage. Hitler made the Germans feel as if he cared personally about each one of them and their lives. Then each of these men stopped doing the very thing that brought them to power.

Alexander the Great isolated himself with a few friends and ignored the hardships of his men. Julius Caesar became captivated with the riches of Cleopatra and Egypt and was no longer engaged with his troops in an intimate fashion. Hitler became a mad megalomaniac who exposed his lack of care for anyone but himself.

The result was that their followers (except for a few sycophants) left in droves. The brilliant comet of their leadership crashed and burned.

Lasting Loyalty

The same thing happens today when leaders fail to exhibit the characteristics that create lasting loyalty.

So exactly what does create loyalty? That's what we are going to explore in this book.

FULL MONTY LEADERSHIP TIP

*Loyalty is what keeps a leader at the head of the pack ...
not to mention alive.*

CHARACTERISTICS OF A NOTABLE LEADER

POINTS TO PONDER From Chapter 1 ...

☼ All notable leaders start out by being genuinely involved and concerned with the people they lead. It's when they stop being involved and concerned that their leadership fails.

☼ Loyalty is what keeps a leader at the head of the pack.

Chapter Two

What Creates Loyalty?

Maybe, like me, you can remember when people went looking for career positions. People looked for jobs where they would (hopefully) enjoy the work, like their boss, learn some new things, and with hard work and a little luck, would advance through the ranks to eventually reach that coveted corner office.

Then again, maybe that isn't part of your experience because you were born in the age of extreme "screen time." Before the extreme "screen time" era, there were not only fewer mobile electronic devices with which to communicate, there was an increasingly rare thing called connection through which we would build genuine relationships.

What Happened to Connection?
Let me show you what I mean. Imagine I ask you if you'd like to go out to dinner with me. As you and I sit down in the restaurant for a relaxing dinner, you look over at a nearby

13

table and see four people sitting together. The table is silent but there's no indication that someone had said something awkward or offensive by which to create this intense silence.

You have a momentary flashback to your childhood and you consider that these "friends" may be praying, as their heads are down and there's no eye contact. Then, the rampantly obvious hits you.

No, of course they are not praying. Each one of them has chosen to go out to dinner with friends, and rather than speaking to the person or persons in front of them, they are choosing to chat with someone who is not there. No doubt, they are telling the virtual friend how boring it is to be out with the folks in front of them. The sad thing is that most often the person on the device does not even fully realize that they are not there in any form other than as a warm body in the room.

Today we have an ever-increasing number of devices by which we can communicate, and yet our communication skills appear to declining at an equally rapid rate. Could there be a connection between this and the fact that the younger end of Generation X and now Generation Y (also known as the Millennials) seem to change jobs almost as often as they change underwear?

According to Gallup Research, "70% of employees are either disengaged, or actively disengaged".

This means they are sitting at their workstations and behaving pretty much the same way as the four folks in the restaurant we just described. Now imagine that instead of just observing these diners being disengaged, you were expected to pay their tab. My guess is that you said (at least under your breath) something resembling "Screw that!"

Yet, this is exactly what is going on in the work world every single day!

Changing Workforce

If you are an executive, you know that the days when companies could expect to have someone come on board with an organization and stay for one long career at that single company have vanished.

According to the most recent data from the Bureau of Labor Statistics, the average worker stays at each of his or her jobs for 4.4 years. That being said, the workforce itself is changing. Many Baby Boomers have reached retirement age; the rest are at least on the brink of it. On average, 10,000 Baby Boomers retire each year. The Generation X work force was smaller and there are fewer of them in the workforce, too. The new workforce is the Millennials (people born between 1982- 2004) and 91 percent of them expect their tenure to be about 1.2 years.

Many studies show that the total cost of losing an employee can range from tens of thousands of dollars to 1.5 to 2 times their annual salary. What's more, as every executive knows, no new employee comes without the need for the company to invest in this individual with some form of training. How much money do corporations and government organizations spend for training? Well, the latest research estimates that American industries annually spend in excess of $100 billion on training and development. That's a lot of money invested in employees who are likely to walk out the door within the first two years.

Two Challenges
So it seems we have two major challenges:

One—lack of loyalty.

Two—when people are on the job, they are not fully engaged.

Both these challenges are brutally hard on the bottom line.

The first challenge costs the organization because of the ongoing need to train new employees. This, in and of itself, has different levels of issues.

First, you and I both know and accept that there will always be a need for training and therefore the investment has to be assumptive. However, when this is the third person you've trained for any given position over the last two years, that is a triple cost (rather than investment) and that can get very hard on the coffers. During that time, there is naturally a loss of productivity, due to the fact that a new person is estimated to take one to two years to reach the productivity of an existing employee.

And hold on—we're not done yet. People are an "appreciating asset," meaning the longer someone stays with our organization, the more productive they are likely to become. This is certainly true at a general employee level; however, all of the above becomes significantly magnified when we are dealing with a top-talent, high-salary individual.

The second challenge with training a new person for the same position is that the budget for new training is usually the same budget as for development, which means that the people who are loyal to your organization may not be getting the development they need in order for them to add greater value to your organization. In case you hadn't guessed it, Millennials leave companies where they don't see the opportunity for growth and development. In fact, 62 percent say they will leave their jobs in the next two years.

Losing an employee after only a year or so not only means wasting precious time and resources on training, but also robs development funds to do so. And again, the investment in training must be a foregone conclusion. However, to lose that employee before the training investment pays off not only depletes the bottom line, it also will, without doubt, deplete something with potentially far greater implications: morale.

Loss of Morale
There are several reason this job-hopping epidemic has such a devastating impact on morale, some of which I will expand on later. However, what I will state right out the gate fits in with my earlier observation about our societal lack of real social engagement. Human beings are naturally tribal; we want to bond and belong. The desire to do so is part of our most basic human survival needs. The feeling that we are part of something bigger than ourselves, where we believe

we are mutually needed and appreciated, is deeply satisfying. Given the opportunity, people will want to attach themselves to a very wide variety of things: their family (or a surrogate family), their pets, their religion and or church, sports teams, and their country. Once that bond is firmly in place, people will, as I am sure you know, do ridiculous things to make sure that bond is not broken. (Including even ignoring facts. E.g., when someone finds out a partner is cheating and refuses to believe it.)

What too few companies and organizations realize and capitalize on is that their employees, at least at an unconscious level, want to feel that same bond with the organization.

It is only in the last ten to fifteen years that companies have begun to truly grasp the importance of brand loyalty and as such have pushed billions of dollars into creating brand recognition. All the while, these companies forget to notice the power of such loyalty when applied to employees.

A Driving Example

A while back, I was mentoring a young man who was a manager at a Mercedes dealership. One day we were having a conversation about the work he does and I asked him if he really enjoyed his work. He told me he did. However, as he spoke I had the sense that he wasn't telling me something. It wasn't as if he was lying or even hiding. I just had an intuitive sense that there was more to this than was being said. It wasn't until we were having a chat about the Jaguar I had just bought that what was missing fell into place.

WHAT CREATES LOYALTY?

You see, I am not one of those guys who know the horsepower, torque, and other "guy stuff" about cars. However, he is. As he was telling me about the (positive) differences between my car and other comparable vehicles, I began to ask him about the car he drove. He told me all the cool things about it and because I knew he worked for Mercedes, I simply assumed that what he drove was just that—a Mercedes. Later on, as we walked outside, we stopped to say goodnight and he clicked the button to unlock his car.

"Bleep, bleep."

My attention was pulled in the direction of the sound to his car. This was a car that even a guy like me, who is not a car nut, instantly recognized as a rather beautiful Audi. With confusion in my voice I immediately asked, "You drive an Audi?"

"Yes," he said, without hesitation.

"How come? Do you not like Mercedes?"

"No, it's not that. It just that they don't offer me any incentive to drive their cars over my Audi."

I stopped for a moment and thought of the huge incongruence of having a manager at a Mercedes dealership driving an Audi, and I had to wonder how short-sighted this company, or at least the dealership, was being.

I decided to take it a step further and ask my protégé a deeper question: "When someone asks you for a recommendation with regards to buying Mercedes or Audi, and assuming the needs they have fit equally, and both cars are in the same financial bracket, what would you tell them?"

Without hesitation, he asked, "While I'm at work, or when I'm at home?"

"At home."

Again without hesitation, he said "Audi."

I wasn't there yet, so I dug a little deeper. "If the company had provided an incentive, would you drive a Mercedes?"

His response was a somewhat surprisingly casual "Yes."

I went on and said, "Same question, only now you're driving that Mercedes ... and someone wants your recommendation. What would you tell them?"

This time he was more hesitant. "Mercedes, I guess."

"How come?"

"Well they are a great car." Suddenly, I could hear irritation in his voice.

Pushing the envelope a little farther, I asked, "Did they suddenly get better than they were two minutes ago?"

"No, of course not," he said, somewhat sheepishly.

WHAT CREATES LOYALTY?

"Then why would you recommend the Mercedes over the Audi this time?"

"I guess I'd just feel that if I'm driving a Mercedes it would be disloyal not to recommend it."

The Reciprocity Principle

What just happened? Why did he go from recommending what he thought was the best car, an Audi, to recommending the vehicle of the corporation he worked for?

Loyalty through reciprocity.

Robert Cialdini, author and seminal authority on persuasion, writes in his book Influence that one of the great laws of influence and persuasion is that of reciprocity.

According to Dr. Cialdini, the Principle of Reciprocity firmly states that we are all bound, even driven, to repay debts of all kinds. Unless we are sociopathic, that moral, socially conditioned debt weighs on us, and so when someone does something for you, you feel obligated to repay. It's an almost knee-jerk reaction.

Further studies have shown that even an undesired gift can generate a "yes" response to a request, even though that initial gift was not asked for.

In his book, Dr. Cialdini cites an example from the '70s: There was a time when you couldn't enter or leave an airport without having a very close encounter of the third kind with a Hare Krishna disciple. Their technique was a simple and powerful use of the principle of reciprocity. The Hare Krishna disciple would simply give travelers a flower and say that it was a gift. And because we all have been conditioned not to be rude, the majority of travelers would smile and take the "gift." The minute that the gift was accepted, the disciple would ask for a donation.

Most people didn't really want the flower and would simply toss it into the nearest garbage can (from which the Hare Krishna would recycle it for the next donation). However, with that pretty flower in your hand, it was hard to refuse a smiling request for a donation. There was built into this "gift" the moral debt of reciprocity. And much of what became a multi-billion-dollar religious empire that spanned the globe was built on little flowers, small donations, and the embedded principle of reciprocity.

Maybe you are saying, "Yeah, but that would never work on me."

Oh really?

Research shows that reciprocity works even if the person you're giving a gift to doesn't like you.

Here's an example most of us have either directly or indirectly experienced. You are mailing invitations to your daughter's wedding and despite your inner struggle, you decide to invite that couple down the street. You don't particularly like them. You don't really want them at the wedding. However, they invited you to their son's wedding a few months ago, so you feel compelled to invite them to your daughter's wedding. Even if you manage to resist sending an invitation, you will likely have to give yourself, and maybe others, all kinds of justification for not having reciprocated.

Even today in our online-driven society, most of us still send Christmas cards. Picture this: Two weeks before Christmas, you get a card from someone you haven't heard from in years. Very often, without even thinking about it, you immediately send one in return. You've already sent cards to all the people who were on your list, and when you were doing it, you may have even thought that you send way too many cards. You may even be pretty sure you'll never see the person you just heard from again— but, they sent you a card, so you automatically send one in return.

The principle of reciprocity is at work in each of these and a million other examples you could come up with yourself.

When one person does something for another, that other person senses that a debt is owed and is compelled to repay. Big or small, we feel the pressure to reciprocate.

Why does reciprocity work? Because we have an inner drive to bond and belong, and reciprocity is one of the glues we use to create that bond.

The Power and Pitfall of Reciprocity
Just how powerful is reciprocity? It's far more than just a polite urge to be nice and play fair. Sociologist Alvin

Gouldner says that there is no human society on Earth that does not follow the principle of reciprocity.[1]

If you truly desire to generate Fiercely Loyal talent in your organization, it must be noted that reciprocity is a deep and powerful principle that, under the right circumstances, is all but impossible to resist and needs to be an embedded principle in your corporate culture.

The formula for using the principle of reciprocity to your benefit is simple: Give something away—a gift, a service, valuable information, assistance, or anything—to create in the other person a feeling of indebtedness. Once the other person feels indebted to you, then you ask for what you want and let the principle go to work.

The challenge with this is that it doesn't take long for folks to work out if the "gift" is a manipulation. On top of that, in a corporate environment you just can't be giving out stuff every day . . . you'd go bankrupt trying to do so. Even more important and potentially dangerous to your culture is that continual "giving" creates the "anti-loyalty principle of entitlement." So yes, reciprocity is an ingredient in building Fierce Loyalty—but it's not the whole enchilada.

---

[1] Alvin W. Gouldner, The Norm of Reciprocity: A Preliminary Statement (American Sociological Review. Vol. 25, No. 2, April, 1960), pp. 161-178.

What's Next?

Let's come back to our central understanding that people want to bond and belong. However, to bond and belong we have to build trust, and that only happens through a psychological sense of safety.

Have you ever fallen in love? If that is so, there's a good chance that at some point you've had the less than pleasant experience of having your heart broken. Now, if you are like most human beings, at that moment you either consciously or unconsciously made yourself a promise to never let yourself get hurt like that again. As a result, when the next person came along you were likely a little less open, a little less trusting, and a little more cautious. However, because of the driving force within all human beings to bond and belong, most people eventually do let someone in—often the wrong person—and, despite the empty promise they made to themselves of "never again," they get used and dumped again.

That being said, you and I have also had the dubious honor of knowing a person who made the same promise of "never again" to themselves and they kept to it. They psychologically built a twenty-foot-high wall with a machine gun post atop it and a crocodile-filled moat at the bottom. The problem is, these folks keep everyone out, including the good people, people with whom they could develop a healthy bond. The result is they become increasingly distant and lonely, because that basic human need to connect is denied. In general, they are usually fairly pissy and not very pleasant to be around.

FULL MONTY LEADERSHIP TIP

*As much as we like to think that the
professional world and the personal world
exist in different realms of reality,
the same basic needs drive us to a
lesser or greater degree,
no matter which realm we are in.*

The Need to Bond

Imagine, if you will, that you are a loyal member of the team and you've been with this organization for a number of years. During this time you have seem multiple people move through the revolving door for a certain position. Even if you are a super warm and friendly person, it's not going to take too long for you to withdraw and begin thinking, *Why should I bother? This person is probably going to leave in less than a couple of years.* A friend of mine had this experience when she went to work at a debt collection agency. People there didn't even know the names of the others in nearby cubicles. When she asked about it, the supervisor said, "We don't encourage people to get friendly. No one lasts that long."

You see, as much as we desire to bond and belong, we also, often unconsciously, behave protectively if we sense a lack of emotional safety. This means that the new person starts in a job and from their perspective, the people at the new job (you) are all very cliquey and unfriendly. The result is silos within silos. Morale goes the direction of yesterday's newspaper and the culture you thought you'd laid out so well begins to crumble, since anyone new (and potentially great) starts plotting their escape within a month of starting at the company.

What Generates Loyalty?

As we have just discussed, losing great people is extremely costly on many levels. So what generates loyalty?

It's one thing for you or me to conduct an interview and ask someone if they are loyal, because they will most likely say "yes." It's a whole different subject when we talk about the demonstration of loyalty.

So let's begin by asking: As a leader, how do you see loyalty demonstrated? Is loyalty demonstrated by your employees getting the work done? Let's face it: employees are not very loyal if that's not happening, because they need to do the work so you can make money, to keep the company that employs these folks in the black.

So one measurement of loyalty is whether people show up and produce. How do you get them to do that? Well, for most of us who own, lead, or run companies that are less than the trendiest companies in the world, we don't have folks banging down our door to do internships. So first and foremost, we must pay them a salary and, depending on the contract, benefits. So now we need to ask, does the old adage of you have to spend money to make money apply? How much pay is required to inspire and generate real effort? Or, to put it another way, can feelings of loyalty be substituted for monetary compensation?

I can think of several circumstances where this might be the case. It can happen when there is massive prestige involved. Bragging rights have value. For instance if someone works for a famous fashion magazine or a prestigious sports team, they might be willing to give up some measure of their income if they can brag to others about where they work. However, bragging rights is only one element required for generating Fierce Loyalty. What's more, if that loyalty is based on prestige, it is not likely to last.

Another way that the feeling of loyalty can be substituted for monetary compensation comes from the feeling of prestige that a person gets from working for, or preferably with, a leader with a big persona and lots of charisma. These are people that others want to be around. During the 1990s, what woman, or for that matter what man, would not have jumped in and worked for free for the opportunity to be with Oprah Winfrey? And despite his horrible reputation regarding his treatment of staff, many people would have lined up all day long to do the same for deceased Apple™ CEO, Steve Jobs. The charismatic flames of such leaders are always bound to attract a certain number of moths, even though the followers may get their wings severely burned in the process.

But charisma and/or persona will only get you so much loyalty. In fact, research is showing that there is an ever-decreasing demand for the charismatic (and often dictatorial) leader.

Please note here that I make a distinction between the charismatic- or persona-based leader versus the "inspirational leader," who also may be charismatic. The first leads out of personality; the second leads out of a deeply considered set of values.

One final way that the feeling of loyalty can be substituted for monetary compensation is when the work itself is deeply inspiring to the person involved. This is how some of the greatest volunteer organizations in the world not only survive, but thrive. However, even the best NGOs can lose great people, people who truly believe in the cause. Inspiring work alone doesn't guarantee undying loyalty.

When looking at generating Fierce Loyalty that is not driven through financial compensation, it comes down to three major elements: Prestige, Charisma, and Inspiration. But is there more?

Money Money Money

Is it important to pay your people well? Yes, of course it is. But how well? And is there such a thing as paying your people too well?

Daniel Pink is an American author who has written five books about business, work, and management. He was also the chief speech writer for Vice President Al Gore. In his book *Drive: The Surprising Truth about What Motivates Us*, he shows that not only does monetary reward cease to motivate us past a certain point, but the increase in that reward actually ends up stripping motivation away.

He says that when it comes to what motivates us, the science is really surprising, and as he put it, a little bit freaky. It turns out that we are not as endlessly manipulatable and as predictable as you would think. He outlines a set of experiments (which I will not go into here; if you want the details I encourage you to purchase his book), the results of which are fascinating.

The first thing he discovered was that as long as a task involved only mechanical skill, financial bonuses worked as

29

they would be expected to—the higher the pay, the better their performance. In other words, if you are paying someone to shovel dirt, the more you pay them, the harder they will work.

There was no real surprise there. But shockingly, once the task calls for even rudimentary cognitive skill, a larger reward led to poorer performance. If people had to think about what they were doing, paying them more didn't increase their performance. What's more is, this was not some single anomaly; in fact, this research has been replicated over and over by psychologists, sociologists, and even economists. How can that possibly be? Well, I'll come back to it in a few minutes.

The folks who carried out the experiments were economists: two from MIT, one from the University of Chicago, and one from Carnegie Mellon—the top tiers of the economics profession. They came to a conclusion that seems contrary to what most of us believed: that the higher the reward, the better the performance. They reported that once you get above rudimentary cognitive skill, it's the other way around. Pink even points out that the whole thing seems like some vaguely left-wing, Socialist idea, or a kind of weird Socialist conspiracy. He also goes on to say that the group that financed the research couldn't be any less Socialist, since it was The Federal Reserve Bank.

Pink goes on to say that for simple, straightforward tasks, traditional kinds of incentives, what he calls carrot and stick, work great! Shovel that pile, get this much money. Shovel those two piles, get this much more money.

But when the task gets more complicated or when it requires some conceptual, creative thinking, those kinds of motivators demonstrably don't work.

Further on, he states that money is a motivator, but in a slightly strange way. If you don't pay people enough, they won't be motivated. However, he says, what's curious about this is another paradox: the best use of money is to pay people enough to take the issue of money off the table.

In other words, pay people enough so they are not thinking about money and they'll think about the work.

Now, here is where Pink reveals the truth of what drives us. He says, once you pay people enough for them not to be thinking about money, three factors lead to better performance—not to mention, personal satisfaction, and, as you will see later on, employees becoming Fiercely Loyal. These three factors are Autonomy, Mastery, and Purpose. Please note that, as a leader who is looking to generate Fierce Loyalty in your top talent, it is vital that you and your organization facilitate all three of these factors.

Autonomy
So what is Autonomy?

People began talking about no longer "working for the man" back in the early 1960s, but just about every one of them ended up doing just that. Why is that? Simply put, because there came a point when they had to think about money. However, that weak rebel's call wasn't so much against the capitalist ideal as it was about having a sense of freedom, and feeling like the captain of one's own ship.

As Dan Pink puts it: "Autonomy is our desire to be self-directed: to direct our own lives."

As I'm sure you are aware, self-direction and autonomy have not been high on the agenda when it comes to traditional management practices. Traditional management was all about compliance; getting people to do what you wanted them to do. In truth, as I have already mentioned, the basic focus of most traditional leadership training is to get people to follow you and have them do what you want/need to get done. Although that may have been perfectly fine in a minimal-thinking, task-based environment, in today's work place, it plain and simply does not work. As a result, we have a leadership crisis and an American workforce that is, for the large majority, actively disengaged. Business Review estimates that the average worker wastes 2.09 hours per eight-hour day, not counting lunch and breaks.[2]

In today's modern workplace, people are doing more complicated, sophisticated things. If you, as a leader, want engagement, you will need to be a leader who supports self-direction—in other words, a leader who encourages autonomy.

Dan Pink gives a terrific example of how handing over direction to the employees adds a ton of value to the company.

---

[2] http://www.businessreviewusa.com/business_leaders/how-much-time-and-money-are-we-wasting-at-work

He cites the company Atlassian, an Australian software company, and the way they do something rather radical. Once a quarter, on a Thursday afternoon, they say to their developers, "For the next twenty-four hours, you can work on anything you want. You can work at it the way you want. You can work at it with whomever you want. All we ask is that you show the results to the company at the end of those twenty-four hours."

Now let's be cognizant of the fact that this is "company time," not free time. Also it's worth noting that this is set up as a fun meeting, with beer and cake and other entertaining things. Now as a leader in whatever form—be it owner, CEO, president, executive, supervisor, or even a manager—you might be thinking, *There's no way we are handing over the keys to these people; they would drive us into the ground.* Well it turns out you'd be dead wrong! That one day of pure, undiluted autonomy has led to a whole array of fixes for existing software and a whole array of ideas for new products for Atlassian that otherwise might have never emerged.

Other top companies that adopted similar policies are finding that they not only work but increase loyalty. LinkedIn has InCubator; this is a program that gives engineers time away from their regular jobs to work on their own product ideas. Apple has Blue Sky, which allows some workers to spend as much as a few weeks working on their own pet projects. Even the granddad of tech, Microsoft, created something called The Garage, a space for employees to build their own products using Microsoft resources.

There was even a time when Google let its employees spend one day each workweek focusing on their own projects, a practice that delivered fifty percent of Google's offerings, including Gmail. Sadly, Google decided it needed that 20 percent time back from its employees and ended the practice. It would be interesting to see how many new and creative offerings Google has come up with since canceling this practice.

Given all this, you may want to rethink your position on whether your people having autonomy is bad or good for your company.

Mastery

Let's take a look at the second engagement factor: Mastery. At one time or another, we have all been in awe of someone who has shown mastery, whether it's a master craftsperson, a musician, a writer, a particular kind of artist, or even the way someone thinks about certain things. We all respond to mastery, and what's more, I believe we all have at least some secret desire for it because it meets some very powerful unconscious needs.

When we have mastery in any given area, there is a far greater chance that we will receive the recognition and acknowledgment we all need and desire. It is from this acknowledgment that we meet our need for significance. Having the need for significance met lets us know we are seen in the greater sense of the word. This, in turn, is one of the ways that we know we have value and therefore we are worthy of bonding with.

Mastery can be tricky, because even though it is possible, mastery is rarely something we are born with. Therefore, if mastery is going to be a path by which we get recognition, acknowledgment, significance, and value, we are going to have to work for it. So for most of us, true mastery not only implies work, it implies consistent work over a long period of time, maybe even a lifetime.

A way to internally define mastery is our urge to get better at something, and then when we get better at it, to see if we can keep getting better. Even though it may make no logical sense, people will play musical instruments for hours each night and on the weekend just to get better. Most of these folks are not planning on becoming professionals, or even hoping to make any money from their skill, yet they toil toward mastery.

Looking purely from the position of economics, an economist would have to ask, "Why are they doing this?" It's awe-inspiringly clear. Working through the challenge of mastery gives us a deeper sense of contribution, and when we combine the desire for mastery with making a contribution, we ignite a deep tribal desire. Once again, we are part of something bigger than ourselves; we belong and we have value. Simply put, we do it because it brings about the sense of personal satisfaction that happens when we overcome a challenge, because it is fun, and most important of all, because it gives our lives meaning—and meaning, as you will see, is vital to creating a culture where your top talent is Fiercely Loyal.

We all know that leadership is at a critical crossroad right now. We are still seeing the old model of dictatorial leadership that makes the personal promise of saving the organization. This of course is massively ego-driven, and it has played out for a very long time, with a lot of success throughout the industrial age.

However, the world and the economy are not what they once were. We can no longer afford to think exclusively of our own needs and greed. We are all part of a global community, and leaders who want a Fiercely Loyal customer base need to show corporate responsibility, community care, and global awareness.

Purpose

As a result, we are seeing more and more of what you might call purpose-driven companies

Back in 1994, Jim Collins, a former teacher at Stanford University's business school, and his co-author Jerry I Porras wrote the New York Times Bestselling book *Built to Last: Successful Habits of Visionary Companies*. They took an in-depth look into eighteen truly exceptional and long-lasting companies and studied each in direct comparison to one of its top competitors.

They examined these companies from their often very humble beginnings. Throughout the book, the authors asked, "What makes the truly exceptional companies different from the comparison companies and what were the common practices these enduringly great companies followed throughout their history?"

Guess what? Among other things, they were all purpose-driven organizations.

Business at its bottom line is about just that—the bottom line. If we don't make money, we are out of business. However, more and more organizations and the leaders within them want to have some kind of inspiring purpose for why they do business. This is partly because leaders are not stupid; they can see the writing on the wall and even though we may be in awe of the massive profits of companies like Monsanto™, not too many of us are willing to reach that financial success by having to live with the title of "the evil corporation incarnate."

Moreover, leaders who have scaled the rocky terrain to climb Success Mountain and are really honest about it know that being part of an inspiring, purpose-driven organization makes coming to work better. It somehow feeds our soul. As a delicious bonus, it's a great way to attract and keep top talent. In other words, purpose-driven companies are another element of generating an organization with Fiercely Loyal talent.

As I just said, the world of business has changed vastly and there is a social and market demand for corporate social responsibility. When it's not there, it won't take long before your customers start to vote with their feet and go somewhere else. As Pink points out in his book, what we're becoming increasingly aware of is that when the motive for profit becomes detached from the purpose motive, bad things happen. Sometimes these are things that are ethically bad, as we saw in 2008 with the financial collapse that clearly came about as the result of a purely profit-driven motive.

The financial collapse was global; however, when an organization is not purpose-motivated, bad things happen in a far more local manner. These include crappy products, terrible service, and negative attitudes in workers at all levels of the organization. The simplicity of it all is that people are no longer going to be loyal to an organization that is purely motivated by profit, and they simply don't do great things in an environment that is uninspiring.

Therefore, to create an environment of fierce corporate loyalty, your people must be aligned with not just some vague mission statement, but rather the overriding purpose you and your organization are aligned with. (Please be patient. A little later, I will explain how "Purpose" and "Mission Statement" are vastly different.)

More and more organizations are realizing this. And here's the news: these are the organizations who will be stealing your star players. Not because they've hired the best recruiters to find them; on the contrary, your star players will simply get up and cross the street of their own volition. Why? Because as we've been discovering, inherently we all want to bond and belong, and there comes a point where we must choose to bond and belong with something deeper and more soulful than the drive for profit.

I believe, and the latest research is showing, that we are at the beginning of a profound shift in both leadership and business in general. There is broadening evidence that the companies and organizations that are going to flourish will be the ones that are driven by purpose.

I said "going to flourish," but make no mistake, this is already fully in process; some people are ahead of the curve and are reaping the benefits because of it.

WHAT CREATES LOYALTY?

Purpose and Profit

Is there anyone living in a first-world country who does not know who Steve Jobs was? I'm sure there are some people, but I think you'd agree they are rare. The reason I bring up the both famous and infamous Mr. Jobs is simple: Meaning/ purpose-driven organizations are already conquering the world of business. When Steve Jobs said, "I want to put a ding in the universe," he was telling you, me, and everyone who worked under the insane pressure he created that both he and Apple Corporation would be driven by purpose first. And, as you may have noticed, they've done pretty well in the profit department, too.

Guy Kawasaki was originally responsible for marketing the Macintosh in 1984 and was known as the chief evangelist of Apple. He said in a presentation he gave in 2004 for the School of Engineering at Stanford University: "The first thing I figured out and learned, sometimes the hard way, about entrepreneurship is that the core, the essence of entrepreneurship is, it's about making meaning."

He goes on to say: "My background is a Macintosh division of Apple computer, and I can tell you with total certainty that we were not motivated by making money. We were motivated by changing the world, to make people more creative and more productive. We were trying to increase the quality of life for the Macintosh user. And that was a great motivation. It kept us going through many, many difficult periods. We were waking up in the morning thinking how we could change people's lives."

POINTS TO PONDER From Chapter 2 ...

- The work force is changing rapidly. The average worker stays at a job only 4.4 years.

- The money spent on training a new employee comes directly at the cost of keeping and developing current employees.

- Lack of loyalty and lack of engagement are two major problems faced by employers today.

- Forming bonds is an essential part of human nature.

- Reciprocity works because of our inner drive to bond.

- Monetary compensation alone does not create loyalty.

- People desire a sense of autonomy in the workplace.

- Mastery is a key factor in keeping employees engaged.

- Purpose-driven companies are both creative and profitable.

Chapter Three

The Importance of Meaning

Meaning is not only what gets people up in the morning, it is what gets them up with a smile on their face and a bounce in their step after having worked late the night before. They want to come back to work for you because they want to be part of something great. And if they feel that they are an important part of the fulfillment of that meaning, they will be Fiercely Loyal to the purpose and in turn your organization.

FULL MONTY LEADERSHIP TIP

As the great Viktor E. Frankl said in
Man's Search for Meaning:

"Don't aim at success. The more you aim at it and make it a target, the more you are going to miss it. For success, like happiness, cannot be pursued; it must ensue, and it only does so as the unintended side effect of one's personal dedication to a cause greater than oneself ..."

Money Isn't THE Answer

We have all had the experience of believing that more money would solve a certain problem and potentially create a greater level of happiness. As leaders, we have in one form or another risen through the ranks, and unless you were directly born into money, as you rose through those ranks, your salary and your general state of wealth also increased. If this is the case, you no doubt had the experience of believing what I just stated: more money will make it all better.

And yet what we all discover is that with an increased income, problems don't disappear; they are simply replaced with a different set of problems. As we grow our organizations, we can come to believe the same kind of thing about our business—this or that problem could easily be fixed if there was more available cash in the coffers. Then as our companies generate more money, we find that we get a whole new set of problems.

Maybe you are the owner of a company, or have been one at some point in time. Perhaps you may have been there at the conception and even birth of a company. If you have been in any of those positions, this will resonant deeply with you. Even if you have never been in that situation, I guarantee that you will clearly see yourself somewhere in this business adventure I'm about to describe.

A Case Study

Lisa had paid her dues and was a well-respected leader in both her company and her industry. She was making great money and, in truth, really didn't want for much. She and her partner had two small children and they had decided way before that happened that her partner would be the primary parent. Life was good!

Well, at least on the outside. You see, Lisa was having trouble sleeping. It was 3:20 am when Brad rolled over in that state where you can still go back to sleep, but you're on the very edge of becoming awake. If everything is quiet and you find just the right position, you'll drift off into a deep slumber and in the morning, you won't remember that you had even seen the clock. But for some reason, as Brad changed position, he became aware that Lisa was silently sitting up in the dark.

"Lise, is something wrong?" Brad asked in a thick, sleepy voice.

Softly, Lisa replied, "No, my love, go back to sleep."

He tried—oh how he tried—and it only took a couple of minutes for him to realize it wasn't going to happen. His eyes were now open and his voice a little clearer. "What is it, Babe? What's bothering you?"

Again, Lisa tried to tell him to go back to sleep and that it was no big deal.

Brad sat up and turned on the bedside light. "Lise, please tell me what's going on."

She took a moment to gather her thoughts before she spoke because she knew what she was about to say didn't really make sense to her, so she certainly couldn't expect it to be understood by anyone else.

"It won't make sense, but it's my work."

As she said it, she wanted to rewind the words. It's the middle of the night, this isn't going to make sense, just shut up and forget about it were the messages screaming at her in her own mind.

Brad immediately replied, "It's your work?" The one-sided light of the bedroom lamp intensified the confusion on his face. "See, I told you it wouldn't make sense."

"It doesn't, because I thought you were really doing well there" "I am. That's part of the problem."

Brad's confusion deepened, and now that going back to sleep was not even an option, he said, "Help me out here. Help me understand so that it does make sense."

Lisa had now turned her own light on and was facing Brad so that they could see each other. "That's the problem; it doesn't really make sense to me either. Like you said, I'm doing really well at the company and I get along with most of the people I deal with. But I'm just not really feeling it."

"Not feeling what exactly?" By the sound of it, Brad's confusion wasn't going away any time soon.

"I'm sorry, my love . . ." Lisa's voice had shifted from the frustrated tone it had had just a moment ago and moved to one of compassion for Brad, who was trying his best to understand something that was still a mystery to her. "I'm sorry, my love. That's the point. I don't really know what it is that I'm not feeling."

THE IMPORTANCE OF MEANING

Brad had known and loved Lisa long enough to know pushing this wasn't going to help. He reached out and, with his arm around her shoulder, he gently pulled her head to his chest. He turned out the light and lightly stroked Lisa's hair until she fell back to sleep.

The following morning was the usual dash before work. Lisa kissed Brad just before she left and told him she loved him and whispered that she was sorry for having awakened him last night.

As far as Brad was concerned, whatever it was that had been bothering Lisa must have passed, because there was no mention of it. But a few times over the next couple of weeks, he woke in the night and Lisa was gone. Each morning, he would mean to ask her where she was, but the mornings were busy, and by the time they were alone in the evening, he had forgotten.

Then one Friday night when they were supposed to be going out, their plans changed. Lisa said, "I'm glad things got changed. I wanted to be able to sit down with you and have an important chat."

The part of Brad that sometimes still felt like a little boy got slightly nervous. He wondered if he had done something that had upset his beloved. But he pushed his fear to the side and put his attention directly on Lisa.

She began speaking somewhat hesitantly. "Do you remember a couple of weeks ago when we had this weird talk in the middle of the night that never really went anywhere?"

Brad knew exactly what she was talking about. "Absolutely," he said.

"Do you remember that when I spoke about work, I said that I wasn't really feeling it, and that I didn't know what it was I wasn't feeling?"

"Yes, I clearly remember that." Brad's face now had a soft smile that invited Lisa to continue.

"Well, I'm pretty sure I know what it is that I'm not feeling and what it is that I want to feel. That's what kept waking me up at night."

Brad suddenly remembered the times when he had drifted out of deep sleep and noticed the Lisa wasn't there.

"Good, what is it?" Brad asked with genuine curiosity.

"Well, I can't really tell you in a specific word, but I think I can explain it now."

"Okay, go ahead."

Lisa now had Brad's full attention. As he watched her speak, he saw in her eye a glimmer of something he hadn't seen in a while. And he took a moment to recognize how lucky he felt that she was his partner in life.

"Do you remember when I started with this company, how excited I was?"

"Yes, of course. I remember us going out for a celebration dinner with Linda and Paul."

"Yes, but do you know what I was most excited about?"

"As I remember it, you were excited because this was a huge jump for you; this was your chance to really prove yourself. Because I remember telling you that you were going to rock this company."

Lisa smiled, remembering Brad's words. "Yes, that's all true, but there was more. I was excited because I thought this company was committed to certain community programs, and I was just as excited about being part of that as I was for the advancement in my career."

"Yes, I remember that now. What happened to those projects?"

Lisa's eyes widened. "That's my point. I advanced so fast, which was wonderful, but I never got to be part of those projects in any major way. And since the '08 crash, they made a bunch of cutbacks on community projects. This is what I mean about not feeling it. For the last few months, when I go to work, I don't have the fire that I once had. That drive is just not there."

Brad felt deeply compelled as he listened to Lisa. He had seen her this way before and he knew that when she was like this, he'd better look out, because things were going to change.

Lisa continued, "At first I thought the way I was feeling might be burn out, but my work load just isn't that tough and I've handled a lot more. I began to question everything, and there are two main themes that just keep coming up. One is that I love my work, but I need it to have a greater meaning than a prestigious title, a corner office, a gym membership, and great pay. Don't get me wrong, these are all great, and I'm really grateful for everything. But I need to find that fire again. The other thing is people . . ."

Brad was once again confused and sure that it was written all over his face. "The people? I thought you said you get on well with everyone you deal with."

"I do, but that's the point."

"You don't want to get along with them?" Brad's confusion was bigger than ever.

"I know it sounds weird, but no, I don't."

Brad was ready to jump in, but before a word made it out of his mouth, Lisa continued.

"I don't want to just get along. Like I said, I want to feel that what I do at work has meaning. I want to be and work with people who are inspired because what we are doing has purpose and meaning to us all. I want to feel that I matter to the people I work with and they matter to me."

As Brad listened to Lisa, he found himself feeling inspired. Lisa's face was lit up, and again he was seeing something in her that he hadn't seen in a while, something he hadn't noticed was gone. But at that moment, he realized that it was the genuine curiosity, joy, and passion he had seen in Lisa in the early days when she spoke of her work. Heck, that was the reason his being the primary parent was an obvious decision. Only now did he realize that all that good stuff had slowly leaked out. Yet just talking about it was somehow filling Lisa's tank again.

"What's more is, I realize that a new job in a new company won't solve the problem—well, at least not for any significant amount of time."

Brad felt like he understood where Lisa was coming from, but there was a justifiable confusion in his voice when he asked, "Well, if you're not feeling it at this company and you know working somewhere else won't solve the problem, what do you want to do?" Before he could finish his sentence, he knew the answer.

"Start my own company."

Not everyone who leaves your team is leaving for the same reasons that made Lisa want to leave her company. She clearly felt that she had attained a certain level of mastery over her position. However, now that the money was not an issue, she found herself desirous of both autonomy and purpose in her career. (I'll tell you more about what happened with Lisa later).

By now, I am sure that you are beginning to really grab onto some of the key elements of what it takes to keep your top talent loyal, and what happens if you don't.

Just let this sink in for a minute—and let's just shift gears and perspective. Let us ask ourselves what loyalty had (past tense) meant to us as leaders, and what we need to be clear about the meaning we give to it now.

POINTS TO PONDER From Chapter 3 ...

- "Don't aim at success. The more you aim at it and make it a target, the more you are going to miss it. For success, like happiness, cannot be pursued; it must ensue, and it only does so as the unintended side effect of one's personal dedication to a cause greater than oneself..."

  ~ Viktor E. Frankl

- Money isn't THE answer to our problems. More money just creates different problems.

- Passion, curiosity, and joy are what get us truly motivated in life.

Chapter Four

Chief Relationship Officer

Whatever your current position is in your organization, I would suggest that you—right here, right now—make the decision to become a CRO. I put it to you that in today's global work environment, in order to be a great CEO, CFO, COO, or C anything, you need to be a great CRO first.

What's a CRO?
So what is a CRO, and why do you need to commit to being one?

A CRO is a Chief Relationship Officer. I will explain in a bit exactly what this is and what it takes for you to become a great CRO. However, the reason why you need to be one is simple: The number one predictor of success, according to Gallup, is the quality of one's relationships—and that means both professional and personal.

I'm sure you are aware that for the most part, people don't quit their jobs. They quit their bosses! Therefore, there's a good chance that in a global job market if you don't become a great CRO, you will start seeing your top talent exit faster than bed bugs off a burning mattress.

Here's why: They (employees) are on to a-hole bosses! The latest research from Gallup shows that, as Gallup calls them, "managers from hell" are creating active disengagement of employees and costing the U.S. an estimated $450 billion to $550 billion annually. Just because your employees are nice to you doesn't mean they don't think you're an a-hole!

Their research goes on to say:

> If your company reflects the average in the U.S., just imagine what poor management and disengagement are costing your bottom line.

> On the other hand, imagine if your company doubled the number of great managers and engaged employees. Gallup finds that the 30 million engaged employees in the U.S. come up with most of the innovative ideas, create most of a company's new customers, and have the most entrepreneurial energy.

Why Good People Leave Good Jobs
A team of Florida State University researchers looked into the idea that people leave jobs because of problematic bosses, and—surprise, surprise! They found evidence that this is a lot more than an idea.

Working with doctoral students Paul Harvey and Jason Stoner, Wayne Hochwarter an associate professor of management in

Florida State's University College of Business, surveyed more than 700 people who work in a variety of jobs about their opinions of supervisor treatment on the job. The survey generated the following results:

* 31 percent of respondents reported that their supervisor gave them the "silent treatment" in the past year.

* 37 percent reported that their supervisor failed to give credit when due.

* 39 percent noted that their supervisor failed to keep promises.

* 27 percent noted that their supervisor made negative comments about them to other employees or managers.

* 24 percent reported that their supervisor invaded their privacy.

* 23 percent indicated that their supervisor blames others to cover up mistakes or to minimize embarrassment.

According to Hochwarter's research, employees stuck in an abusive (professional) relationship experienced more exhaustion, job tension, nervousness, depressed mood and mistrust.

They also were less likely to take on additional tasks, such as working longer or on weekends, and were generally less satisfied with their job. Also, employees were more likely to leave if involved in an abusive relationship than if dissatisfied with pay.

The Party Line

Research shows that employees who leave of their own volition generally do so because they've formed a very different perception of their leader, employer, or organization from that of the official party line. Unfortunately, it is rare for an executive to create a safe enough environment to facilitate a team member to openly speak of such incongruence. It takes an authentic (Full Monty) leader with vast courage and minimal ego to face such situations with the grace to dig deeper and find out what part of the company's or the leader's story isn't ringing true.

Let's face it: it's far easier to make it all about them and shrug off people leaving the company as unimportant, or to pretend they never happened. The problem is that, over time, not only will your talent pool have gotten very shallow, but this is the world of social media. You can bet your back teeth that those leaving will tell others about the lack of congruence.

Not the NICE Boss

Let me share a secret with you: becoming a great CRO is not as simple as becoming "The NICE Boss." In many ways, being a great CRO is contradictory to being nice. In fact, one of the principles we teach at The Authentic Speaker Academy for Leadership is that, to be a great leader, you MUST become a master of dealing with conflict. The challenge comes when we try to apply outdated conflict resolution techniques that all too often can leave individuals feeling frustrated and compromised. It's for that reason that I will give you some very specific Full Monty conflict resolution strategies a little later in the book.

For now, what I'd like you to do is flash back into your memory banks and remember when you had someone who was just perfect join the organization and then turned out to be less than perfect. Now please note, I am not talking about someone who had proved himself or herself over a period of time. I'm talking about someone you professionally fell in love with very early on in the hiring process. (As you will soon see, I use the term "fell in love with" for good reason). I realize there have been people who you "loved" right away and they worked out great, but what we are talking about here are the ones you absolutely loved who, somewhere in the range of twelve to twenty-four months, you realized you couldn't stand. Remember that one—those ones?

Do you ever wonder why someone can go from being the person you pinned enormous hope on to someone you can't wait to get rid of, in such a short time? Well, the answer may surprise you. It's not just you who experiences this; in fact, it's not your fault. It is part of the human condition. As you read on, you will immediately realize that this is not just a professional dilemma; it is one of life's dilemmas.

Potential
Psychologically speaking, there are several stages to relationships. Again, these apply to both personal and professional; all relationships have stages.

Stage One of any relationship—whether it's with a potential new romantic partner, a therapist, a coach, a boss or a golden employee—is called the "romantic phase." The romantic phase of relationship in general tends to last approximately twelve to eighteen months (although it can be shorter). During this time, we tend to see the very best in the other person. Obviously, this is not true for everyone we meet. However, it is true for those we feel a great pull toward. That pull is an "attraction," and attraction is not limited to romantic relationships, but rather it's related to *potential*.

When we (consciously or unconsciously) see something in another person that we think/feel will fill a perceived gap in what we need, it is a natural response for us to begin to become infatuated with that person. For the most part unconsciously, we start projecting our hopes onto that other person. There are many challenges with this, not the least of which is that the person we are projecting all this onto may have no real desire to step into that potential. Of course, if they don't step into the potential we see in them to the degree we have ordained as the appropriate amount, we become disappointed in them and often just want to remove them from our lives. Conversely, we will fight for them, saying that we know they have what it takes if they will just step up. All too often, the disappointment and ensuing resentment just keeps building.

Is this starting to ring any bells for you? Can you let yourself admit that you have done this at some point in time? Well again, I remind you, you are not alone; we have all done it!

We all have vast and untapped potential; however, if we measure someone's intelligence by their ability to do things we want them to do but they have no real interest in, then we may all be seen as fools in any particular context.

Power Struggle

As the romantic phase of any relationship starts to come to its end, we begin entering Stage Two of relationship. This phase of relationship is called "the power struggle."

One of the sad things about contemporary society is that we have come to see hitting this phase of a relationship as a sign that the relationship has come to its end. In truth, an Authentic Vulnerable Full Monty Leader understands that this is where the real relationship can begin. That is why an Authentic Vulnerable Full Monty Leader is committed to becoming a master at facing, dealing with, and resolving conflict.

However, before we start looking "out there" at what we can do for—or with—"them," you should know that mastering conflict starts with understanding what triggers conflict within us. I will go into the specifics of how to do that a little later on. However, what I will tell you up front is, you will have to confront some of the old ideas you have about what it takes to be a leader.

FULL MONTY LEADERSHIP TIP

*If you are afraid of the power struggle,
you will not only prolong it, you will make it
more difficult to move to the next steps.*

The Next Stages

While every relationship, both personal and professional goes through stages, the next stages are less applicable to becoming an Authentic Vulnerable Full Monty Leader than to personal relationships, so we will not go into detail about them. If you are interested in learning more, check out my book *Don't Read This, Your Ego Won't Like It.*

Finally, before we go on to talk about the characteristics of a CRO, let me plant this seed and see how it grows as you continue reading:

Your Vulnerability is Your True Power!

CHIEF RELATIONSHIP OFFICER

POINTS TO PONDER From Chapter 4 . . .

- ☀ A CRO is a Chief Relationship Officer.

- ☀ A CRO is the most important officer in any company that wants to succeed in today's business world.

- ☀ People don't quit their jobs. They quit their bosses!

- ☀ Research shows that employees who leave of their own volition generally do so because they've formed a very different perception of their leader, employer, or organization from that of the official party line.

- ☀ To be a great leader, you MUST become a master of dealing with conflict.

- ☀ The first two stages of all relationships are: Potential and Power Struggle. Every relationship, personal or professional, goes through these stages.

- ☀ Your Vulnerability is Your True Power!

Chapter Five

Courage and Vulnerability

A s I pointed out in the last chapter, to become effective
CROs, we must commit to becoming vulnerable leaders. However, for most of us who sit, stand, and operate in
leadership roles, vulnerability seems to be the pinnacle of
weakness. The very idea of displaying weakness is enough
to justify closing this book . . . that is, unless you are smart
enough to understand that some of what were the best practices in leadership yesterday are some of the worst practices
today. One of the ways you will know this is to see with your
own eyes that the number one most troubling issue for 75
percent (and increasing) of CEOs is human capital—namely,
keeping top talent!

Real Courage Requires Vulnerability

Despite what you've been taught, vulnerability is the very opposite of weakness; in truth, it's all about courage. Make no
mistake, for someone to be truly courageous, vulnerability
must come first.

I made the conscious decision not to title this book some version of "the courageous leader" because in many ways, courage can be faked. What's more—and I'm sure you know this as well as I do—when we fake courage, we may still get the applause and the garlands placed around our necks that honor us as heroes, but we will still secretly feel like cowards.

One of the ways we can fake courage is by doing something that others see as scary, while we are so rehearsed at it that it creates no challenge whatsoever for us. For example, we may gasp at the aerial performances in the Cirque Du Soleil, but for the members of the troop, it is pretty much just their job. For a stunt person, part of the thrill is convincing you and me that the dangerous- appearing action is actually dangerous. It doesn't require any real courage.

On the other hand, real courage requires vulnerability. Real courage requires us to step into something where we cannot predict the outcome; something that, in some way, seems terrifying, not because we could die, although that may be part of how we feel, but because we feel we might receive the most painful of punishments—that of being rejected, disowned, and ultimately isolated.

That's why I tell you that real courage cannot exist without the risk of vulnerability!

The Requirements of Relationship

It is the nature of human beings to be in relationships, and even the greatest of leaders is not a lone wolf—because if she or he were, there would be no one to lead.

COURAGE AND VULNERABILITY

Just take a moment and think about it; the challenge is that leading requires relationship, and relationship requires other people, and other people, as you know, can say and do things that hurt us (even if we are presenting an impervious persona). Therefore, to be a great leader, you must become masterful at relationships by embracing vulnerability and finding a way to bring vulnerability and courage together, not only in yourself, but also in all those who surrounded you. Such an act requires real intimacy—and there is no real or lasting intimacy without raw, honest vulnerability.

Of course, I realize that, after reading that paragraph, there are some folks who have already slammed this book closed. Some may have even hurled it across that room, followed by saying (either out loud or in their heads) something resembling; *"What a piece of crap. I am a lone wolf. I don't need anyone. I'm not afraid of being rejected; everyone knows that about me."*

Let me just say that if a moment ago you were that person and you just picked the book back up, thank you for giving this book another chance. Here's why: I want you to know I get it! I have been there. I have been the person who looks like no one can hurt me. But the truth is, like you, I am human, and despite the armor I have worn at different stages of my life, I have been hurt by others. The challenge is not in discovering how to avoid getting hurt; the challenge is in deciding that the person who hurt you does not represent every human being on the planet.

Throughout this book, you will see that many of the messages we have received about leadership that may have been somewhat relevant before are the very same messages that will have you fail miserably as a leader in today's world. Particularly damaging are those messages that suggest, or demand, that leaders stay on their pedestals and keep their professional distance.

You have no doubt worked under and heard those old-school leaders repeat the rhetoric that people are their greatest assets, and yet you have seen those so-called leaders behave in complete contradiction to that message. These leaders are disengaged from their people. By keeping "professional distance" and calling it conservative business etiquette, they tell themselves it's okay. Meanwhile, their star players are covertly or overtly doing a mass exodus.

Individuals as Individuals

If we genuinely understand that our people are our greatest assets, then as forward-thinking leaders, we must become masterful at dealing with individuals as just that: individuals.

What does this mean? It means that, despite what we've been taught about keeping ourselves separate and making sure we don't allow people to break the chain of command, we must get down in the trenches and get to know our people. We need to understand what matters to them. This is way beyond the "open door management" of the past. This is about seeing the humanity of people, having them see your humanity, and coming at your personal and business relationships from a place of genuine caring.

Many years ago, I was trained as a counselor/therapist.

COURAGE AND VULNERABILITY

Very early on in that training, I received one fundamental tenant regarding what it took to be a great therapist: the insistence upon our keeping professional distance. That meant as therapists, we were supposed to stay emotionally distant from our clients (I never liked or used the term "patients" as it implied sickness.)

To be completely honest with you, I was never able to do it. When my client was in pain, I felt that pain. When they had success, I felt their joy and celebrated their success along with them. And despite my original educators' insistence that being emotionally invested would impair my ability to help, the evidence was completely contradictory: I was a highly successful and in-demand therapist with a significant waiting list.

In the beginning, I thought that I should feel bad about caring so much, and I even wondered if I had made a good career choice because of it. Then, fortunately for me, I read a book that was first published in 1978, written by an ex-military psychiatrist. The book wasn't specifically about how to be a better therapist; however, it did dramatically impact my approach to the work, and it removed the guilt I had carried about how I did what I did.

This book was *The Road Less Traveled* by bestselling author M. Scott Peck. The book sold somewhere in the region of seven million copies in the US and Canada alone. It was and is filled with what I believe are brilliant insights and strategies. However, there was one piece that remains with me to this day, and as much as it impacted my therapeutic style, that same piece has profoundly impacted my leadership style, too.

Here's the excerpt:

> "If the psychotherapist cannot genuinely love a
> patient, genuine healing will not occur. No matter how
> well credentialed and trained a psychotherapist may
> be, if they cannot extend themselves through love to
> their patients, the results of their psychotherapeutic
> practice will be generally unsuccessful.
>
> Conversely, a totally uncredentialed and minimally
> trained lay therapist who exercises a great capacity
> to love will achieve psychotherapeutic results that
> equal those of the very best psychiatrists.

I know, I can hear you: *What the heck does psychotherapy
have to do with leadership?* You may even be saying: *I have
absolutely no interest in being the therapist for anyone, let alone
someone on my team.*

Good news! I am not suggesting that. However, there is
a lesson here for the leaders of tomorrow, and to make
it clear, I will rephrase Dr. Peck's words into a leadership
context:

If a leader does not genuinely care about a team member, genuine loyalty will not occur. No matter how well
established and or trained that leader may be, if they
cannot extend themselves through genuine compassion,
empathy, caring, and vulnerability, the results will be that
their team will never know the fruits of lasting success
and they will be generally unsuccessful in the ways that
will matter most.

Conversely, a totally untrained or minimally trained leader who exercises a great capacity for genuine compassion, empathy, caring, and vulnerability will achieve bottom-line results that will equal and often exceed those of the most established leaders.

It is the capacity for genuine compassion, empathy, caring, and vulnerability that will define the leaders of tomorrow. But to have those qualities takes far more courage than to be a dictatorial, distant leader.

Moreover, authentic caring, compassion, empathy, and vulnerability can only be genuinely delivered by a leader who has had the courage to "take a look under their own hood." Only a leader with genuine self-awareness can have real awareness of another. Only leaders who can be honestly vulnerable and compassionate with themselves can have genuine compassion for others. Such a leader not only attracts great people, but those people become Fiercely Loyal.

A Leader Goes First

I believe that great leaders have the ability to inspire us, and nothing is more inspiring than leaders who walk their talk.

In 2005, I was invited to speak at a global sales conference. I don't often get the opportunity to do last-minute gigs, but that is exactly what this was. An executive I was mentoring at the time had apparently been speaking with someone they knew at this company and found out that their speaker had bailed. My client recommended me.

The gig was going to be taking place at the end of the week, and I had a rather unusual opening in my schedule. There seemed to be a synchronicity that made it work, so when the call came, I took the opportunity.

Because I did not have my usual prep time, I only knew the most basic of information about this company and that it was a global sales conference. Arriving at the venue that morning, I have to tell you, I was expecting a considerably larger group. But no matter. I was introduced to the global sales team leaders, who each ran their own division in different countries. I was also introduced to the CEO, a man by the name of Graham Kill. Graham clearly had the poise of a leader, while at the same time the people around him seemed to have an obvious respect for who he was as an individual. Graham seemed both grounded and approachable, and I took an instant liking to him.

As I finished my presentation, Graham approached me and thanked me; then he asked if I would like to join the team for dinner that night. I was honored, and I replied that I would. Entering the restaurant, I was motioned by Graham to sit next to him. After a day of team-building exercises, my morning presentation, and the first sips of wine, everyone was in a great mood, making for a dinner that was lots of fun for all.

During dinner, Graham and I got to know each other a little better by getting into some very meaty discussions about a range of subjects including our thoughts about leadership and personal leadership styles. I clearly remember a point of real rapport came as we both spoke of how the foundation of great leadership was reliant upon self-knowledge and the necessity to lead one's self. Graham, being a true leader, had done some self-inquiry. However, as a quality leader, he understood that there's always another level of depth. He began to inquire about the strategies and processes I offered. We spoke about how I could come in and work with his C-suite executives, and how I have worked with companies who were discovering the power of Vulnerable Leadership in generating Fierce Loyalty in their own teams.

Even though he can be very playful, Graham is a fairly cool, calm, and collected kind of guy, with a James Bond-esque demeanor. In his calm but nonetheless warm manner, he began to inquire whether I did this kind of work one-on-one or only with teams. I shared with him that I have an exclusive and extremely intensive process where I work one-on-one with a leader. This process is called The Personal Excellence Architecture for Leaders and it requires that individual to be with me exclusively, without interruption of any kind, for up to twenty-four hours straight. It requires a level of open vulnerability that most people, let alone leaders, are unfamiliar with. Following that initial process, there is a further six months of mentoring and coaching for integration.

As you can imagine, that level of intensity alone is enough to sort out those who are genuinely committed from those who are merely interested. It clearly shows which true leaders are all about action and which are just interested—"the tire kickers" who will have a myriad of reasons why they can't do it.

Within a week, I received a call from Graham saying, "Let's do this thing." Within a month, we had set up to meet on neutral ground on his way back from some other destination and go through his PEAL (Personal Excellence Architecture for Leaders).

I won't go into the specifics of the process, and I can't share what Graham discovered. However, what I can tell you is that Graham became both deeply aware and extremely mindful of the beliefs and thought processes he had been having and the behaviors he had been doing that were either limiting or expanding him: the things that were either creating distance and disengagement or connection and engagement with others. And now he had the tools to focus on and use to move toward the latter.

The following summer, Graham brought us into Europe to work with his executive leadership team, who were flown in from their different countries. This would be my opportunity to see the true level of integration Graham had applied around those he was leading. In the lead-up months before, Graham and I had discussed the outcomes he was looking for. Right at the top of the list was something so many leaders in his position face challenges with: silos.

As a company grows, it's natural to go from everyone wearing multiple hats and communicating about everything, to the development of departments and teams. As exciting as this can be, one of the most common challenges is that internal departments become adversarial, in essence building silos around themselves. As a result, departments stop communicating with each other. Graham had made it crystal clear that he wanted me to find a way to pull the silos down and open up fluid communication between departments and the leaders within them.

As we set up that morning, Graham and I took some time to sit and catch up. He asked me, "What can I do to assist so that this training will have the best possible outcome?" My answer was short and to the point: Leaders go first! So when asked to be vulnerable and open up, leaders go first and lead by example. Without hesitation, Graham agreed to do so, and then did it. In doing so, he assisted me in creating the safety needed for his executive team to embrace the power of vulnerable leadership. People began opening up about the challenges they faced with their teams, with each other, and most importantly, with themselves.

However, it should be noted that this was not about finger-pointing at others or even self-berating. This was about vulnerability. So when a team member was struggling with another team member's way of being or leadership style, instead of making the other person wrong, the first person voiced it as their own challenge, a challenge that they themselves were responsible for resolving.

At the end of the five-day retreat, not only were the silos down, but each person felt they genuinely knew the other members of the team. It went further; certain members of the team who had simply resigned themselves to the idea that they would never get along with another particular team member found themselves connecting so deeply with that person that they felt like this was someone they trusted, respected, and even considered a friend.

Caring, Compassion and Vulnerability

As I said earlier, the capacity for genuine caring, compassion, and vulnerability will define the leaders of tomorrow. As much as one of the major roles of a leader is to inspire and motivate people, that inspiration will wear off faster than a fake tan in a bubble bath if the leader has not had the courage to go through—and continue to go through—a process of self-inquiry. In other words, they must be willing to look under their own hoods.

By virtue of that, it was Graham's willingness to get comfortable being uncomfortable as leader and step forward into the power of vulnerability with me, and then his team, that made what we did a raving success, every bit as much as my leadership of the group. Why? Because genuine courage is contagious.

FULL MONTY LEADERSHIP TIP

Self-knowledge is the cornerstone of emotionally intelligent Leadership. Commit to becoming brilliant at working out why you are actually upset about any given situation. (Alternatively, get help in learning how to do so).

Emotionally intelligent leaders don't play the blame game, nor do they let rambling, negative self-talk take control of their minds. Make finding your drivers, motives, and moods an adventure. Search for clues that reveal why you feel the way you do, and what you can do in order to come to peace with whatever it is.

Leadership is Uncomfortable

As Seth Godin writes in his book Tribes: We Need You to Lead Us, "Leadership is scarce because few people are willing go through the discomfort required to lead . . .. It's uncomfortable to stand up in front of strangers. It's uncomfortable to propose an idea that might fail. It's uncomfortable to challenge the status quo. It's uncomfortable to resist the urge to settle. When you identify the discomfort, you've found the place where a leader is needed. If you're not uncomfortable in your work as a leader, it's almost certain you're not reaching your potential as a leader."

Again, only a leader with the courage to face the massive discomfort of looking into his or her own darkest places can have real awareness of another. And only leaders who have done so can be truly compassionate with themselves and, in turn, have that same genuine compassion for others. All this springs from the birthplace of vulnerability. Such a leader not only attracts great people, but those people become Fiercely Loyal, because loyalty has many components. One of the most important ones is emotional safety.

Creating Emotional Safety

Michael told me that he had come out of the meeting with Lynda shaking his head. "Maybe it's just a silo thing," he told himself. He figured that Linda and her department were being overprotective and unwilling to communicate openly with other departments. Deep down, though, he knew the truth: there had always been tension between Lynda and him, even though it was clear that they both believed they had enough leadership skills to reach being C-level executives.

Nonetheless, Michael secretly thought Linda was a bit of a bitch, and often found himself calling her that in the safety of his own mind, and as such, working together was becoming increasingly difficult.

From Michael's point of view, Linda refused to compromise on anything. After that last meeting with her, he was beginning to consider the offer he had received from a headhunter. He didn't want to leave the company. He really liked what they were about, he just didn't know how to deal with Lynda. And you and I both know that people rarely leave "companies" but rather bosses—or, in this case, a co-worker.

Lynda, on the other hand, as so often is the case, had a very different perspective. From her point of view, there was more at stake than personal opinions; she was committed to the vision, mission, and purpose of this organization. After all, those were the things that had won her over and had gotten her to leave her former, very well-paid position. She felt that the minute anyone in the company began compromising on those things was the minute she would begin to look elsewhere. And that minute might just have arrived during that last meeting with Michael.

Why should you care about Lynda and Michael's challenges? Because, as I've pointed out, the Number One challenge for top executives is loyalty. In other words, getting the super talented to stay with the organization is the single most difficult task facing those at the top.

Much of this challenge is, I'm sorry to say, a leadership issue. Because whether we admit it or not, leadership forms culture, and a leader who has not embraced the power of vulnerability is not demonstrating real courage, and in turn is generating a lack of emotional safety.

So, let's take a look at one way a very well-intentioned corporate culture can end up falling apart.

Fear of Conflict is the Root of Resentment

On my radio show (The Authentic Leadership Show) I had the honor of interviewing many outstanding leaders, one of whom was a hard-core trial lawyer turned peacemaker who specializes in difficult, complex, and intractable conflicts. His name is Doug Noll.

You can find the interview here:

http://fullmontyradio.com/leadership/doug-noll-full-monty-leadership-radio

In that interview, Doug and I spoke about the misconceptions of peace. One of the subjects we covered was how carrying a fear of conflict actually ends up creating resentment, and resentment is a precursor to escalated conflict. Resentment becomes an underlying cancer that will eat away at the fabric of your organization's culture. Once the fabric of your culture begins to erode, you are going to have major problems keeping your best employees.

Before we go any further, I want to set something straight. To have a healthy corporate culture that has an ongoing momentum of growth, healthy conflict must not only be encouraged, but your team must be trained in how to facilitate healthy conflict amongst themselves and with those they lead.

When members of a team have not been given a way to have healthy conflict, they begin to disengage even from an organization they truly believe in, as was clearly illustrated in the earlier example of Lynda and Michael.

Number One Fear

We've all heard the fear of public speaking is the number one fear people have, right? Well, you know what? I don't believe it. I am the president of The Authentic Speakers Academy for Leadership, and we have had everyone from top corporate executives to self-employed moms in the program, and getting them over the fear of public speaking is far easier than getting someone to face any real conflict. Fear of conflict, much like stage fright, has its root in a fear of rejection, and creating a safe place for conflict means, by its very nature, creating a safe place for innovation.

I realize that you may never have considered that fear of conflict is massively detrimental to both the creativity and growth of the individual. However, once you grasp that, it's not much of a logical leap to realize that the stunted growth of the individual will, in turn, stunt the growth of your team and ultimately the whole organization within short order.

In the simplest of terms, what's happening with individuals is going to impact the entire organization.

That's where authentic, effective, and vulnerable leadership plays a major role.

The fact is, a leader must have an effective strategy to health-ily deal with conflict. What may surprise you is that we at Authentic Paragon Alliance have found that developing healthy conflict skills not only deepens understanding and generates a greater bond between the individuals involved, but it also creates a greater bond to the organization.

Another name for that bond is Fierce Loyalty!

Again, this means that you and I must have the courage to not only face, but also walk the conflict all the way through to resolution. To do this, we must face one of our most basic human fears: the fear that we are not good enough. You see, if we don't face the conflict, we can hold onto the idea that we were "right." Whereas, if we face the conflict, we may discover something else altogether; the "not good enough" monster rises up from the dark depths of our being, and in that mo-ment, it can feel like it will consume us.

The interesting thing about human beings is that we are driv-en to connect; we want to belong. It is out of this deep desire that we behave in ways that we tell ourselves will create con-nection, while what many of these behaviors do is the exact opposite: we end up feeling deeply disconnected.

The conversation in too many people's heads goes something like this: If I face the conflict, I may be wrong; if I'm wrong, I will have revealed my flaws; and if I reveal my flaws, peo-ple will leave me. This in turn drives the desire to be perfect, which has its roots in the conditioning that who we are is not good enough. And so, we strive to be perfect, in hope that we will be good enough to be accepted, valued, and in turn, loved.

The problem is, even if we actually get to claim the 100 percent and are told "it's perfect," the glory is at best fleeting, and once again we are left to doubt our value and, in turn, our lovability.

It is only through the courage of stepping up into vulnerability that we discover our true and intrinsic value.

Misconceptions About Vulnerability

Right here we must address a few misconceptions about vulnerability. First off, despite what you've been taught, vulnerability is NOT weakness. As alluded to earlier, it actually is both power and strength. And later on, I'll show you exactly how this is true.

Furthermore, one of the great misconceptions about vulnerability is that it means flagrant disclosure to anyone and everyone about our deepest insecurities, wounds, dreams, and desires.

This is NOT healthy vulnerability. Healthy vulnerability includes healthy boundaries. In fact, in my experience, too much disclosure often is another way of hiding, meaning that a person who does that is often nothing more than someone who is mired in their history and using that history to not allow you and me (or even themselves) to truly see them. Very often, such a person believes that they are being vulnerable and authentic because, most often, they are curled up on the floor like a human snot ball. That may, indeed, be a form of vulnerability; it is however NOT the of kind healthy vulnerability we are referring to here.

Corporate Culture

Okay, let's get back to looking at corporate culture and how it can feed the "fear of conflict" that so often lies at the root of loyalty issues. The challenge is that what a leader thinks their corporate culture is and what it actually is are often two very different things! As different as apples and hamburgers!

Jumping in a little deeper . . .

What is corporate culture, and how does it relate to dealing with conflict and creating loyalty?

Corporate culture is many things. However, at its core, it is how people think and act in relation to the organization.

It's what will get you chastised or applauded, praised or damned, promoted or fired.

Yes, it is set of a spoken or unspoken rules, or codes of conduct.

I'm sorry to say, your corporate culture will fall apart when the people involved do NOT have a safe place to express who they are, and this is particularly true when dealing with Millennials. Sadly, this in turn erodes trust, and as you may or may not know, trust is one of the primary elements of high productivity.

Just think about it, and you'll see it makes perfect sense. When the members of your team don't feel safe to speak their truth, they are not safe to explore new or innovative ideas. When there is no safe place for vulnerability, people cannot be open or honest with each other. When there is no trust, people simply don't produce their best work. It's as simple as that! Without a strong foundation of trust in your corporate culture, you end up generating a subculture (that will eventually become dominant). This subculture will, in all likelihood, become at the very least silently adversarial in nature, and thus it becomes politically driven rather than innovation- and growth-driven. As a result, the team begins to disengage; self-preservation replaces innovation and commitment fades at lightning speed.

If you want a corporate culture in which individuals, their ideas, and the organization flourish, as a leader who is in turn developing leaders, you MUST develop a way to facilitate healthy conflict. If you don't, nothing else you do will make much difference.

A healthy corporate culture needs to be an internal representation of both the vision and mission of the company.

So here's the tough question ... if you are honest enough to answer it. What's your corporate culture? Is it a safe place for the expression of the individual, or are people shushed?

COURAGE AND VULNERABILITY

POINTS TO PONDER From Chapter 5 . . .

- ☀ "Fear of conflict" is detrimental to the growth of your organization. Authentic, effective leaders must become masters of vulnerability and conflict resolution and help those they lead to develop those same skills.

- ☀ What your corporate culture is and what you think it is may be very different, so find out the truth.

- ☀ When your team does not feel safe expressing who they are, trust will fall apart.

- ☀ When your culture is not based on trust, ideas and innovation become repressed.

- ☀ Lack of trust in a corporate culture generates a subculture (that becomes dominant) that will be, at best, silently adversarial at worst openly agitated and aggressive.

- ☀ For individuals, their ideas, and the organization to flourish, your corporate culture MUST have a way to facilitate healthy conflict and its resolution.

Chapter Six

A Culture that Generates Fierce Loyalty

Chances are, if you are reading this book (which obviously you are), you are a leader. Maybe you are even a leader who understands that to be the best you must keep adapting and growing. In all likelihood, you've been a leader for a long time, and as such, your organization has what appears to be an established culture. However, the question that must be answered is, do you have a culture that actually generates Fierce Loyalty?

To answer that question, we have to take a step back and look at some of what we outlined about what it takes to generate Fierce Loyalty in your people. Earlier we spoke about what drives people and keeps them engaged. I shared with you the need for your people to have a genuine sense of autonomy as well as ways for them to develop mastery, and of course, the need to do meaningful work in a purpose-driven organization. A culture that generates Fierce Loyalty must have those things as its backbone.

If your culture demeans any one of those areas, I'm sorry to say, your culture over the long haul is not one that will generate Fiercely Loyal talent.

Number One Priority

If I were to pick the number one priority from the previous list, it would be for the people working for you—whether they are your superstar leadership team or the janitor—that you facilitate those people doing meaningful work. Therefore, the natural question that springs forth is, how can you make sure that your people are doing meaningful work?

The answer will appear simple on the surface, but for you to apply it so that you have a culture that generates Fierce Loyalty will require some digging.

To help you, I am going to set forth some questions. However, to do this, I am going to have to assume that you are a top dog in your organization, meaning you have the power to, if needed, make sweeping changes. (If you are not that person, these questions will allow you to see if you are indeed working in the right organization for you to experience not only the success but also the fulfillment of doing meaningful work.)

Important Questions

First question (this needs to be answered without checking your literature): What is your organization's mission statement?

Write down your answer here: Our Mission Statement is:

_____

_____

_____

_____

_____

_____

_____

_____

Next question: What is the organization's vision statement?
Write down your answer here: Our Vision Statement is:

_____

_____

_____

_____

_____

_____

_____

_____

_____

Next: What is the Purpose Statement of this organization? Write down your answer here: Our Purpose Statement is:

_____

_____

_____

_____

_____

_____

_____

_____

Now assuming you answered those three questions without checking with anyone else, (by the way, many leaders have already hit a blank), we move to the next level of questions.

Assuming what you wrote down is the correct Mission Statement of the organization: What do you see as an active, day-to-day demonstration of this mission statement?

The active, day-to-day demonstration of our Mission Statement can be seen in/through:

_____

_____

_____

Assuming that what you wrote down was the correct Vision Statement of the organization: What do you see as an active, day-to-day demonstration of this vision statement?

The active, day-to-day demonstration of our Vision Statement can be seen in/through:

_____

_____

_____

Assuming that what you wrote down was the correct Purpose Statement of the organization: What do you see as an active, day-to-day demonstration of this purpose?

The active, day-to-day demonstration of our purpose can be seen in/through:

_____

_____

_____

At this point, you may have hit a wall in that you may not have been able to fully answer the first set of questions regarding the mission, vision, and purpose of your organization. But if you did make it past that point without checking, you may have gotten stuck on the second set, the day-to-day demonstration of these things.

All too often, an organization's mission statement is something that was manufactured during a weekend retreat, with its highest intentions being that it resembles what we are about, it's easy to remember, and it's cool and catchy. This, my friend, is not going to generate Fierce Loyalty. Then when it comes to vision and purpose, far too many organizations have a vision; however their purpose is very often little more that to be the biggest and the best. Again, this is not the stuff that will create a fire in the hearts and souls of your people.

I'm sorry if you are struggling at this point; however, please remember, my intention is to assist you in becoming a world-class leader whose organization generates Fierce Loyalty. For that reason, I'm going to ask you to take up your pen and go another level deeper in answering the next set of questions.

Digging Deeper
Okay, you ready? Take a breath and let's dig in . . .

Assuming that the organization is profitable and is continuing to be so: What is the number one most important thing to this organization?

Write down your answer here: The number one most important thing to this organization (after profit is taken care of) is:

_____

The next question is simple and not too surprising:

What are the active, day-to-day demonstrations that this is indeed the most important thing to us (the organization)?

_____

_____

Strapping on the tanks to dive a little deeper—ask yourself: What is the number one most important thing in life to me?

You know the drill; put your answer here:

_____

If I had that taken care of and it was rock solid, in that I don't have to worry about it—what would be the next most important thing in life to me?

_____

And if that were totally taken care of, what would be the next most important thing in life to me?

_____

And if that were totally taken care of, what would be the next most important thing in life to me?

_____

And if that were totally taken care of, what would be the next most important thing in life to me?

_____

Okay, we are now five levels deep. When we work with executives and teams, we take this even deeper, but for now, we will stop there. Having those five levels clearly laid out should give you a reasonably clear insight into your personal maxims.[3]

_____

[3] Maxims are personal and should not be confused with values. Values are most often societally conditioned and based on what we have been told/taught is right. Maxims tend to be more honest in that they come about as more of a subjective, emotional response.

At this point, it should be clear to you whether there is a clear alignment with what you believe your organization's maxims are (as revealed by mission, vision, purpose and the day-to-day demonstration of these things) and what you have discovered yours are.

We tend to think that asking ourselves deep and meaningful questions is a little too esoteric and out of touch with business, when in fact, asking yourself the kinds of question laid out here is the ultimate business strategy in that it allows us to remove distraction. It allows us become aligned in all our endeavors and, at least as important, it take us from what so often becomes empty success to a deep sense of purpose and fulfillment.

I put it to you that, particularly as a leader of self and a leader of others, your life is worth examining. If this is true, then it is not only valuable but also vital that you take a sincere look at the meaning of your life.

FULL MONTY LEADERSHIP TIP

The questions I have laid out above are designed to assist you in discovering the deeper meaning and purpose of, not only your organization, but also what truly matters to you.

I will go so far as to say that when these two are aligned, that's when you will truly know a whole new level of joy as a leader.

There is one proviso here, and that's this: the meaning of your life is just that—the meaning you give your life. If you (consciously or unconsciously) took on a meaning for your life that's making you miserable, you may want to dig a little deeper and create new meaning.

I know for sure that, in my own life and in the lives of the leaders I mentor, looking at and designing the meaning of life has had a profound impact on the quality of our lives. Emphasizing your meaning will bring you greater levels of joy, significance, success, and fulfillment.

Bringing Your Leadership Team on Board
I would highly suggest that at this point, you give the same set of questions to your entire leadership team.

Supposing that they do actually know what the Mission, Vision, and Purpose of the organization is, this exercise will give you a clear insight as to whether your organization is generating Fierce Loyalty.

If your leadership team's maxims are aligned with the organization's maxims, what you have is a team of people who are doing what they feel is meaningful, purpose-driven work with an organization they trust.

Several years ago, we were brought in to work with a leadership team in the UK. They were all good people doing great work within the organization. Early on in our work, I decided to take a temperature reading of the alignment of these folks with the organization they worked for.

I asked each of them to simply write down what they believed the company mission statement was, without consulting or sharing anything with their peers. One by one, I asked them to stand and read out what they had written, making sure that the CEO would go last. As each of them stood and shared, I would glance over at the CEO and see the look on his face. By the time we were half way through the team, the CEO looked like he had steam coming out of his ears. When we finished that exercise, we realized that the only person of this International organization's leadership team who actually knew something as simple as what their mission statement was, was the CEO. Needless to say, at that point, he was not a happy camper.

How can we expect genuine loyalty and not just lip service if our team doesn't even know the mission statement, let alone how to be aligned with it?

Knowing What Really Matters

To have a Fiercely Loyal culture, we, as leaders, cannot be afraid to polarize people. This means we must be crystal clear ourselves on who we are and what matters to us as an organization. This way, we will quite naturally repel those who are not in alignment with our purpose, mission, and vision. Just as clearly, you will naturally attract top talent who are aligned and will become Fiercely Loyal, because working with your organization will be both meaningful and purposeful.

I should clarify at this point that, in designing an organization's corporate maxims, we must be highly cognizant of the fact that, if a maxim is truly a maxim, and if a company's purpose is truly its purpose, it will remain so, no matter what. This means that despite shifting markets, business trends, or what your competitor is doing, your purpose is your compass, always pointing to your true north, and your organization never abandons that.

POINTS TO PONDER From Chapter 6 ...

- ☼ A culture that generates Fierce Loyalty must give its people a sense of autonomy, ways to develop mastery, and meaningful work.

- ☼ Everyone on your team must know, understand, and be able to articulate the company's Mission Statement, Vision Statement, and Purpose Statement, as well as show how these are demonstrated in day-to-day actions.

- ☼ Polarization is part of generating Fierce Loyalty. When leaders are clear on what their organization is all about, they will repel those who are not in alignment with that purpose and attract those who are.

- ☼ Maxims are personal and should not be confused with values. Values are most often societally conditioned and based on what we have been told is right. Maxims tend to be more honest in that they come about as more of a subjective, emotional response.

Chapter Seven

Why Purpose Matters More Than Profit

Here's what we know: Over the long haul, purpose matters more than profit! The real bottom line is, only sixty-seven companies that were on the Fortune 500 list in 1955 were still there in 2011. In other words, companies that almost anyone would have said were rock solid back in 1955 had either gone bankrupt, merged, gone private, or fallen off the Fortune 500 list altogether, just fifty-six years later. Therefore, it's probably safe to say that many of today's Fortune 500 companies will be gone and replaced over the next fifty-six years.

Why do you think that 87 percent of the Fortune 500 companies that where around in 1955 were gone by 2011?

The answer is Purpose! Companies that are purpose-driven last. If you don't believe me, go back and read Jim Collins's book *Built to Last.*

That Purpose has to be at the very core of any company that is going to endure. This is particularly true when considering that both your general work force and upcoming leaders will be Millennials. For Millennials, as I will clearly show a little later, the number one driving force in the work place is meaningful work.

The Cost of Being Purpose-Driven

Doing business this way will, without doubt, generate Fierce Loyalty in both your employees and your customers. That being said, it should be noted that there is a cost to doing business this way. One of the major costs is that, If your organization has not been authentically purpose-driven, there's a good chance there will be considerable growing pains. Moreover, operating from a place of purpose first will work as a filter. Some people (including some already in your organization) will be repelled and others will be dynamically attracted. Some people who were just with you for the paycheck will suddenly come out of the woodwork and really show you their skills, because they are inspired by the purpose of the organization.

I've been in business a long time, maybe longer than some of my readers have been on the planet. In that time, I've been asked many times by those who are considering going out on their own about the cost of doing business. It seems that people want to, if they can afford it. The answer, particularly today, isn't as simple as it once was.

The Real Cost of Business

Obviously, no matter how big or small your organization is, there are some basic costs like the cost of the property you operate out of (although many folks are starting businesses out of their own home). There is the obvious cost of staffing, although with remote workers, many of those costs can be reduced. Then there are fixed costs such as electricity, phone line, Internet connection, etc. And on top of that, there is the cost of marketing. If people don't know you exist, it's very difficult for them to buy from you, right?

However, I put it to you that those aforementioned things aren't the real cost of doing business in this global market place.

So let's get into the real meat and spuds of it.

There is another cost that you will want to consider seriously before going into business, or for that matter genuinely stepping up to be the kind of leader required in today's marketplace. It's a cost that will become more and more evident in the new economy.

Let me warn you: It's a cost you must seriously weigh before you make a commitment.

As you can no doubt tell, there are still signs of the old-guard, cutthroat, massively competitive business and leadership model around. This old model may even have legs—for a little while longer. But mark my words, those legs are getting more and more wobbly by the moment.

The great news is, there's a new model for doing business that is emerging. It is a model that I believe will challenge the heck out of the old guard, because it will require a complete overhaul of how we do leadership.

At the center of this new model of business and leadership is a theme that today's generation will come to expect, both as members of your team and as customers. It will need to become a central and very necessary cog for doing business from here on in.

What is the cog?

Responsibility and caring.

Let me be clear, this isn't the old corporate rhetoric of saying "We care." No, what I'm talking about here is actually, genuinely giving a shit about the people who work with and for you and the people you do business with.

Facebook, Twitter, LinkedIn, YouTube, and social media in general, have changed the distance between people. These sites have allowed people who were once vague icons off in the distance to become people you can reach out to in as little as 140 characters—and surprisingly, they will, and most often do, reach back.

Today's rock, pop, and movie stars are brought to the top through the relationships they build online. Tomorrow's business will be built in just the same way. Make no mistake, it's already happening!

So when you ask me, "What is the cost of doing business?" I'll tell you ...

It's 1:43a.m. right now, on a work day, and I'm writing this to YOU—for you, yes YOU! Why? Because I genuinely give a shit!

The real cost of doing business today is that you must genuinely care about and be willing to be in relationship with your employees, team members, and customers. As an Authentic Vulnerable Full Monty Leader, you must choose to treat them with the respect of being people rather than "underlings" or "buying units."

If, in fact, the research is correct and CEOs are four times more likely to be psychopathic than the rest of the population at large, these changes will certainly do a lot to reveal them.

The Bottom Line

If you don't want to be genuinely relational, then you, my friend, cannot afford the cost of doing business today, no matter how much money you have!

One of the foundations of becoming an Authentic Vulnerable Full Monty Leader is that you must become genuinely relational. If you think this is some kind of marketing phrase, or rhetoric you can throw around at the leadership retreat—think again.

To be genuinely relational, you have to be willing to do what it takes to show someone you genuinely care, even if there is nothing in it for you. The companies that are willing to see past the immediate bottom line will, without doubt, dominate their markets and in turn create Fiercely Loyal customers and employees.

A Case Study
Take a look at Patagonia.

Back in 2011, Patagonia, Inc., a California-based clothing company focusing mainly on high-end outdoor clothing, launched a first-of-its-kind campaign for a consumer products company: it asked customers to reduce unnecessary consumption of its own products.

I hear you: *What ... have they gone mad?*

"The Common Threads Initiative addresses a significant part of today's environmental problem − the footprint of our stuff," notes Yvon Chouinard, Patagonia's founder and owner. "This program first asks customers to not buy something if they don't need it. If they do need it, we ask that they buy what will last a long time—and to repair what breaks, reuse or resell whatever they don't wear any more. And, finally, recycle whatever's truly worn out."

Patagonia, in turn, committed to make products that last, help repair quickly anything that breaks, and recycle the company's entire product line.

To help customers put used clothes back in circulation, Patagonia and eBay have joined forces to launch a new marketplace for customers to buy and sell used Patagonia gear. (No profit for Patagonia.)

The campaign flies in the face of conventional retail and economic theory that stresses the importance of ever-increasing growth.

In September of 2013, Patagonia announced its latest campaign, called The Responsible Economy, and outlined its numerous environmental and social "firsts" since being founded forty years ago.

Rick Ridgeway, Patagonia Vice President of Environmental Affairs, said: "Patagonia's mission is to 'inspire and implement solutions to the environmental crisis.' There are two vital concepts in that statement: we implement our own solutions and we inspire others to follow our lead."

Patagonia is a company that clearly exemplifies what it means to be both a purpose-driven organization and a genuinely relational one.

Maybe you still have your doubts. Maybe you can still hear the echoes of the board shouting about shareholders, profits, and bottom line.

The Rest of the Story

Well, I've only given you part of the Patagonia story. According to a Bloomberg Business Week Article, in 2012—which included about nine months of the "buy less" marketing—Patagonia sales increased almost one-third, to $543 million as the company opened fourteen more stores. Last year, revenue ticked up another 6 percent, to $575 million. In short, the pitch helped crank out $158 million worth of new apparel.

Meanwhile, Patagonia founder and owner Yvon Chouinard has estimated revenue will continue to grow about 15 percent a year.

The strategy works for generating profits, meaning, and the Fierce Loyalty of both employees and customers—and that's what it's all about.

To reiterate: the real cost of doing business is that you must be willing to be in genuine relationship with your employees, your team and your customers. Simply put; you must be willing to genuinely give a shit.

FULL MONTY LEADERSHIP TIP

Those who go into business to make money rarely get anything else.

The single most important tenet of business used to be competition. Find out who your competition is and destroy them . . . right?

Well, not anymore. At least, not if you want to stick around.

The new model is one rooted in The Four C's, and that's where we are going in our next chapter.

WHY PURPOSE MATTERS MORE THAN PROFIT

POINTS TO PONDER From Chapter 7...

- Purpose matters more than profit.

- Purpose must be at the core of any company that endures.

- To become a purpose-driven organization will entail growing pains.

- The real cost of doing business is becoming responsible and caring about your team, your customers, and everyone you come into contact with.

- If you don't think you can be profitable and relational, read about Patagonia.

- Those who go into business to make money rarely get anything else.

Chapter Eight

The 4 C's:
Cooperation, Collaboration,
Contribution, and Community

What if you, as a leader, operated as if your organization were unique in the marketplace? What if, instead of being focused on how to destroy the competition, you were focused on your mission, purpose, vision, and your clear points of differentiation? How much more focused could you and your team be? If you got competition out of the way, there would be so much more energy available for you to be more creative and innovative—and as a result, you could focus a lot more on the 4 C's that could take your organization to new heights.

Look, I know the idea of "no competition" sounds crazy; maybe it even sounds like some extreme Socialist dream. However, what I am referring to is quite the opposite of a Socialist agenda. I am not going to go to deep into it here, except to suggest that you grab a copy of a groundbreaking book by perceptual positioning expert Stephan Stavrakis called The Only. Once you move the idea of competition out of the way, you can really focus on the four C's.

Cooperation and Collaboration

Let's take a look at the first two of the C's—Cooperation and Collaboration. Cooperation suggests that we take a look at those we may have previously seen as competitors and see if we can find a way for us to cooperate that will benefit both parties and potentially our customers.

Competition is pervasive in our culture, and as much as it can push us to be better, it also can be a very sharp, double-edged sword. When thinking about Cooperation, it may be useful to consider the world of software development and open source projects. Developers participating in the same project are often the same people who would be in competition if this were a proprietary project. These same developers working in open source usually cooperate at levels that are higher than those they demonstrate in proprietary software projects, and it's often due to internal competition. In such a situation, the design phase is usually completely open, with all developers collaborating. During the coding phase, it is quite common for a developer to read and fix bugs in the code being developed by another, without any animosity.

I am told that the flow of information on such projects is usually very high, and problems are solved by consensus rather than by one person competing for glory, status, or financial gain. All of this collaboration, in addition to being more effective, usually causes the developers to be more committed to the project, and it makes their work much easier.

As a leader looking to be an Authentic Vulnerable Full Monty Leader, I would suggest that you take a look at whom you personally and organizationally have considered the competition, and consider how you might cooperate and perhaps even collaborate to add value. You may be very pleasantly surprised by the outcomes.

Intrapreneurship

Another area where cooperation and collaboration can work is internally, within your own organization. As I spoke about earlier, departmental silos can be devastating to the culture, creativity, and morale of an organization. One way to bring down the silos and create stickiness for your top talent is to develop an intrapreneurial environment.

An intrapreneur is encouraged to focus on innovation and creativity and is given the space and resources to transform ideas into profitable ventures while operating within the organizational environment. Intrapreneurship allows, even facilitates, those people within your organization who are innovative self-starters to behave like entrepreneurs while still working within your organization. Such an environment allows an individual to create a team to work on projects they want to develop—and you, the organization, get the benefits.

This is particularly powerful in generating Fierce Loyalty in your top talent in that, as mentioned before, a key driver in Millennials is the desire to develop mastery. An intrapreneurial environment allows them to do that without the risk of going it alone.

Contribution and Community

Now let's take a look at Contribution and Community, as these are major forces when it comes to keeping Millennials Fiercely Loyal. If you want to keep your top Millennial talent, you'd better be doing business from a standpoint of making a difference. That also means producing products or services that people love so much that they rave about them to everyone they know. If an individual works for you, they are proud to say they are part of your organization, because they are certain that your organization cares about what it is doing.

Contribution and Community must be tied together because, as an organization wanting Fiercely Loyal employees and customers, you will be reliant upon the dialog that can only take place in an authentic community.

Committing to develop your community is far easier said than done. However, I promise that if you want to truly stand out as an Authentic Vulnerable Full Monty Leader, and you want your organization to have real longevity, it will be essential.

Failing to create Community in today's market place of social media means that you will essentially be deaf to the voices of your fans and your critics, and that's a price no company that wants to stick around can afford.

In the online world of social media, a company can no longer sit back and throw out marketing campaigns telling the consumers who they are. The Mad Men world of advertising is over! In today's marketplace, you as a leader need to have your ear to the ground, because a very vocal complaint is no longer someone who writes a nasty note to the company and in return receives a form letter saying, "We'll look into it." In today's world, the comments go viral and such an incident can blow up in a leader's face so fast that it can take him or her down quicker than a wrecking ball.

A Case Study in What Not to Say

Back in late 2013, such an event happened to a highly successful business leader. Interestingly, this was a leader who had indeed built a Fiercely Loyal community, but because he did not authentically and compassionately, (and that's the key) have open dialog with them, he fell from grace faster than a fundamentalist minister caught in a gay love triangle.

Chip Wilson, the founder of the global sensation Lululemon, had one of those foot-in-mouth moments we've all had, only he had his during a Bloomberg TV interview. Bloomberg's Trish Regan asked Chip about the fact that there had been a lot of talk about how Lululemon products seemed to have gone down in quality and that their yoga pants were "pilling" and becoming "see-through."

Chip responded with a comment that I'm sure he wished he could have wound back time the minute it came out of his mouth: "It's really about the rubbing through the thighs, how much pressure is there over a period of time, and how much they use it."

As you might imagine, there was an online firestorm about Chip's statements that did nothing less than scorn him and his judgment of women whose thighs rub together.

The next day, Chip did put out an apology.

Sadly, it sucked!

I'm sorry, but who ever worked with Chip to prep him did a crappy job! They (if there was someone advising him) did not understand the power of social media and online community.

To me, this was a golden opportunity for Chip and Lululemon. However, that's not what happened. Chip Wilson's apology ignored the offended customer and was directed entirely at the Lululemon employees. Big mistake!

Let me give you an inside track on this. Like most people in business, I'd heard of Chip Wilson through people we had in common, but I had never met him—until one brisk, Northwest day.

We were both bundled up pretty good, because although it was nice and sunny, it was also cold. Chip and I crossed the street from Starbucks, where we had met up, and walked the shoreline of the beach for our forty-five-minute walk/meeting.

We spoke about many things, including the coaches and consultants he had brought into his company to assist its growth to the next level. Chip even took the time to ask me what I thought I could bring to the company. We spoke about the fact that he was excited about the new leadership team they had put in place. I asked him what it was like to hand over a company he had birthed to a board of directors, since the company had gone public, and he was quite open and frank about his loss of influence. I sensed a slight sadness.

With a background of thirty years in psychology, leadership, and the behavioral sciences, I consider myself a good judge of character and a profiler of what drives people. (Sometimes it feels like I'm a bit too good at it, because I can I see stuff I'd rather wasn't true. Of course, over time, what I see in the shadows usually finds its way into the light.)

During our conversation, I could feel that Chip wasn't one of those people who feels instantly comfortable with others. He didn't strike me as a natural "people person" and even seemed a little socially awkward to me. However, in all fairness, we had never met before and he didn't know me from a bar of soap, so why should he have been comfortable?

Although he didn't come off as a particularly warm and fuzzy guy, he was clearly driven by something bigger than "financial success." When he spoke of his company, there was passion and purpose in his voice, maybe even love—not so much of the entity itself, but rather of what he felt the company stood for, and certainly of the people and the culture there that is, by some people's standards, cult-like.

As I said, Chip had a genuine love for the culture that I believe he was instrumental in creating, and as much as I sincerely appreciate that he apologized to those who suffered the backlash of his comments—his staff—he missed the mark with the Lululemon Community. His apology needed to connect with the customers, too, the people who put money in the cash registers of the Lululemon stores, which allowed the people who work there to keep their jobs. The offended customer needed the apology, and if Chip would have delivered that, this whole thing could have been turned into the chance of a lifetime.

I just wish I could have whispered where to go next ...

If, after being confronted by the interviewer regarding the quality of the product deteriorating, he had of said something in the region of:

"... and as such, it's true that the quality of our product has suffered. And I want to say to you—we let you down, and I personally take responsibility. I am genuinely sorry! And I will be meeting with my board to make it right with you. You have been faithful customers, we appreciate you and your belief in Lululemon, and we are going to make this right."

If Chip had said something of this sort, he would have shown himself as the true and authentic leader that I believe he wants to portray. I also believe that this whole thing would have had an entirely different outcome, because it would have shown some of the key ingredients for generating Fierce Loyalty: honesty, compassion, transparency, vulnerability, and accountability. Such a statement may have even built on the previous Fierce Loyalty of the brand!

Within one month of delivering the incomplete apology, Lululemon Athletica named a new chief executive and billionaire Chip Wilson was out of the company he founded, all because he did not have authentic, compassionate dialog with the people in the Lululemon Community.

Non-negotiable Goal
Community and open communication with your community are vital. To do this, you as a leader must decide on a daily

basis that, come what may, having a Fiercely Loyal community is a non-negotiable goal. Just as important is to remember that this is a two-way system; just as you are working to have your team develop open, authentic communication with your community, you and your team must be willing to do the same with each other.

Some of the key elements of building a Fiercely Loyal community are that your corporate mission, vision, and purpose are openly communicated, as are the organization's maxims. Doing this will galvanize the bond. Remember, people want to and need to bond. By genuinely displaying and openly communicating about your corporate mission, vision, purpose, and maxims, you give them clear and emotionally relevant reasons to bond.

Having an open, communicative community will tell you more about your customers than a million-dollar market research ever could. It's important to make sure that the community isn't all about you (the organization). The focus should always be on the community itself. Think of Unilever's product Dove and their campaign for real beauty. The British newspaper The Independent said: "It's an ad, but Dove's Real Beauty campaign is a game-changer!" These ads went viral at supersonic speed. In the three-minute advert (which Time Magazine described as a mini-documentary), an FBI-trained forensic artist sits behind a curtain, unable to see the subject, and draws a portrait from the subject's self-description, which astonishingly results in skewed, caricature-esque sketches.

Then that same artist draws a second portrait of the same women using only the descriptions given by strangers. This results in a much softer and more realistic picture of the person, and is in turn a massive awakening to the subject regarding the poor self-image they held. *

Let's be perfectly clear. Dove is a subsidiary of Unilever, and like all other companies, it wants to make a profit. However, by following up these viral ads with community sites online and actual live, off-line community events where they are listening to the pain and needs of their community, Dove has become a trusted brand that cares.

The Advantages of an Authentically Focused Community
Community is becoming a hot subject right now, but if it's not done correctly, the customer and even your own team will see through it pretty darn quick. However, an authentically focused community brings specific and very distinct advantages that will give you clear point of unique distinction from those who you may have previously considered your competition. Not least of all, it will provide a truly honest, grassroots research and even development team who will tell you what they want and who will be hungry to buy it from you, because they feel like they were on the team that created it. Of course, you will have happy customers who, because they are members of your community (membership should have its privileges), will be empowered evangelists for your organization.

But again, make no mistake: this is not an arm's length kind of thing. You will have to get down and be transparently

---

* Even though I'm clear that what Unilever did was brilliant marketing, I believe it also made a huge difference in the self- esteem of the participants (and potentially viewers). Simply put, they added value to their community.

vulnerable. You'll have to tell them what you are struggling with and that you need their help, and when they give it, you'd better listen and let them know that you are listening.

FULL MONTY LEADERSHIP TIP

*Building a community is no different
than building any relationship . . .
the other person has to know that they are
genuinely important to you
and that you "get" them.*

Here's the truth: I don't actually know how or why you became a leader. However, you got here, and I'm betting that a part of what gets you through is the difference you get to make. One of the ways you and I get to know we've made a difference is when people are happy as a result of what we've done and where we've led them.

True Happiness
According to some very recent scientific research into what makes us happy, scientists have discovered that more than wealth, or even pursuing the things that we believe will bring us pleasure, what really makes us feel truly happy and fulfilled is the engagement and connection we experience with others. Let's put this in the context of business and more specifically loyalty: quite simply, there are customers and prospective customers out there who are looking for ways to engage and connect with you, your people, and your organization, and

what's more, they want to engage and connect with each other. Denying them this not only denies you, your team, your organization, and these prospective customers a bond, but also a sense of belonging and ultimately real happiness.

Bottom line: much like creating a bond with your team, when your customers begin to see your organization as a source of happiness and fulfillment, it will be very difficult for them to leave you!

The big takeaway here is this: When it comes to community, always remember, it cannot be about your organization; it's always got to be about the people in that community and how you can serve them (even if it's with something you don't directly offer).

THE 4 C's

🔆 The 4 C's: Cooperation, Collaboration, Contribution, and Community—are key to taking your organization to heights you've only dreamed about.

🔆 If you want to attract and keep Fiercely Loyal employees, you need to do business from the standpoint of making a difference in the world.

🔆 Failing to communicate with your community can lead to disaster. Take Chip Wilson and Lululemon as an example.

🔆 Community and open communication are vital for a successful business.

Chapter Nine

What If?

I can hear some of you now: You know what, this whole philosophy of Authentic Vulnerable Full Monty Leadership is really making some rock solid sense to me, but what if...?

It is a perfectly natural response of a discerning leader to ask "What if?" What if . . . this whole idea of loyalty being tied to trust and vulnerability is just some passing trend? What if . . . this is not practical in an organization of our size (because we're so much larger . . . we're much smaller . . . than the companies Dov usually works with). What if . . . we lose some of our "best" people?

I'm sure some folks will come up with a whole lot more . . . So what if? Let me share some political history with you, and then you can draw your own conclusions.

The Hawke Effect

We have all seen enough sensationalized "news" to know that when personal improprieties start leaking out of a politician's personal life and into the public domain, it can be a very fast and slippery slope from fame and favor to disgrace and disrespect. When Australian Prime Minister Bob Hawke's family problems splashed over into the political domain, he was extremely close to a complete personal and political collapse.

Bob Hawke was first appointed to the Australian Council of Trade Unions, and after a decade at ACTU, he was elected to the House of Representatives as a Labor MP. I tell you this because I want you to have a view into not only the man but also the image. Bob Hawke was seen as, as the old adage goes, "a man's man." He was clearly in touch with the working man. And although he was a bright, well educated, and articulate man, he always came across as a man of the people.

While his wife Hazel stayed in the background, running the house and rearing the children, it was well known that Hawke worked hard, drank hard, and played hard. (He was, looking back, the personification of the good Aussie bloke stereotype.)

Hazel, despite the verification of the rumors, was a down-to-earth woman who kept her emotions under firm control and had no illusions about her husband's wandering eye and other body parts.

Reportedly, neither of them was particularly happy in the marriage; however, the household worked around the dysfunction—that is, until it couldn't.

120

WHAT IF?

Bob and Hazel had three children—Susan, Stephen, and the youngest daughter, Rosslyn. Rosslyn was an adorable toddler whom it appears was very close to her dad. In the blink of Australia's history, she had grown up to be a quick-witted and pretty young lady who looked a lot like her mom had in her youth. In one newspaper report, Rosslyn had once said with great humor after having her hair and make-up done professionally for a party: "Don't touch me! I'm a work of art!" It seemed that everyone doted on her and none more than her dad.

Peer pressure is a powerful thing, and something most parents are pretty powerless against, and in the early 1970s in Australia, like most first-world countries at that time, a huge number of schoolchildren were experimenting with marijuana. Hazel, having discovered that both her daughters were smoking dope, approached the issue as a progressive parent, encouraging them to be open rather than secretive about it. Hawke disapproved of marijuana, which he had never tried. However, he had no moral high ground to stand on, as his own drinking was legendary. Pot and the use of it by the girls became another one of those family issues that would get pushed under an ever-growing carpet.

By the time Rosslyn had reached fifteen, she had left school and home for what was described as a gypsy life in the drug houses of Australia's metropolis, Sydney. Hawke and his wife Hazel lived in total denial that Rosslyn was a troubled kid who was now living in an environment where the transition from pot to taking hard drugs was certainly no great moral leap.

However, as time passed, there came a point where there was no denying that their once quick-witted and pretty young daughter had become a ghostly waif. Hawke snuck under the radar; he went searching for, and eventually found, Rosslyn in a squat house in a Sydney lane.

At that time, Bob Hawke, "the man's man," was arguably the most significant political figure in Australia. Therefore, it was decided that Rosslyn's teen-aged indiscretions would become a family secret. She regained her lovely appearance, and married a young man from a respectable family and presented her parents with their first grandchild, a son. On August 1, 1984, she gave birth to a second son. The Hawke family image was intact—or was it?

In the meantime, Rosslyn's elder sister, Sue, who was living in Japan at the time of the 1983 election, had returned to Australia and had become very active in left-wing political activism, and guess what? She had recently been convicted of possession of marijuana.

The issues with Sue may have taken the Hawke's eyes off Rosslyn and her husband; however, it was obvious to everyone who knew them and partied with them that they liked to party hard. There was no doubt that they were using heroin. It seemed that everyone in their circle knew what was going on—everyone, that is, except her parents. Hawke and Hazel clung to the belief that their daughter was clean and did not use hard drugs. They clung to it more tightly than a shipwrecked guy clings to a life raft.

The call came, and with it a reality check that would sever both illusion and denial from reality as swiftly as a guillotine separates a head from the body. The hospital said that

WHAT IF?

Rosslyn, a new mother, was so completely wasted on heroin that she could soon be dead.

Here was Bob Hawke at the height of his political power, a man who had risen so high that he was parenting the direction of his country, who was now clearly a failed parent and guardian of his own children.

Hawke told only a few of his most intimate friends what was going on, and no one else on his staff. Nevertheless, most noticed that something was wrong; the usually vocal and charismatic prime minister was unusually quiet and was clearly distracted and nervous. He began to sink deep within himself.

By the beginning of September 1984, a public storm about drugs was brewing; this would be the moment that would bring the convergence of Bob Hawke's private life and the national public interest together in a head-on collision.

Although it wasn't officially on the schedule, the general election was imminent ...

Opposition leader Andrew Peacock had found, he believed, a site from which to launch an attack on the prime minister. He publicly accused Hawke of undermining the fight against the drug trade, of protecting "some of the most powerful criminals in Australia," of being "a perverter of the law" who "associates with criminals and takes his orders from criminals."

Hawke marched out of the chamber in fury. Little did Peacock know that, if anybody hated drug dealers, Hawke did. In response, Hawke threatened legal action if accused outside parliament of criminality.

The National Times had picked up and run a story that the prime minister's elder daughter, Sue, had a drug conviction that by now had been overturned on appeal; this insinuated corruption of the legal process. Hawke was beginning to look like he was going down faster than a lead balloon.

At a press conference a week after Peacock's censure motion, a journalist asked Hawke about the fact that he had threatened Andrew Peacock with legal action and questioned Hawke if he saw this as making a mockery of the political system.

With television cameras trained on him, the facade began to crack. Hawke replied, "In public life you cannot, it seems to me, entirely abandon the rights that you have, because it is not only a matter affecting yourself." The eyes of this once hard-nosed "man's man" became filled with tears as he continued. "You don't cease to be a husband. You don't cease to be a father. My children and my wife have a right to be protected in this matter."

It felt like the Australian nation held its breath as tears began flowing down Bob Hawke's cheeks. A reporter turned to him and asked if he was upset by The National Times article about Susan. Now openly weeping, he replied, "Of course I was, because like any father, I love my daughter. I trust her, and she was completely exonerated by the processes of the law. I had no contact with the judge or anyone involved in it, and yet you have this insinuation that affects her. Of course, I'm upset."

The question had referred to the legal situation of his eldest daughter Susan, but for those who knew, there was little doubt that Hawke had answered thinking of his younger daughter, Rosslyn. He later said that he was thinking of her day and night. He was also deeply concerned about how to save her and his grandchildren, who could soon be motherless.

The press conference was the fuse that lit the dynamite of a full-blown crisis in the political office. Hawke, after a month of silent self-beratement, could no longer conceal the family secret. Nor could he function as national leader.

He apparently went directly from this heart-wrenching interview to a meeting with Mahathir Mohamad, the man who was the Malaysian Prime Minister at the time. Mahathir Mohamad had hanged people for possession of heroin, and Bob Hawke once again burst into tears, weeping in Mahathir's arms as he told him the story.

When Hawke called his staff together to explain what was going on, they were more annoyed than compassionate. The prime minister had buckled; the man who had been a political rock was crumbling before their very eyes.

In a flash, Hawke's personal and political lives were colliding, and there was nothing he could do about it. Prime Minster Hawke's office and staff were slow to realize that he had fallen into a deep dark depression. They had been so used to him being an impenetrable rock that nothing could shake that they were virtually blind to the reality of what was in front of them. How long his depression lasted is contested. However, what we do know is that Australia's leader had, during this time, contemplated some pretty dire choices: resignation or suicide.

During this time, the intensity was not letting up; both of his elder children had become political, but not as their father might have preferred. Both were now strongly left-wing in their sympathies, especially Stephen, who had argued bitterly with his father over uranium and uranium mining during the ALP conference two months earlier.

By September 1984, the government called for an early election. At the end of the night of December 1, when the votes were counted, Bob Hawke and his government were still comfortably in power, with a sixteen-seat majority.

The breakdown that Andrew Peacock and so many others thought would destroy Bob Hawke certainly took him out of the realm of being a political god. Yet, I can clearly remember sitting in my living room watching one of those news shows where they go out on the street and get public opinion about a given issue. This time, when the Australian people were asked why they voted for Bob Hawke after everything had been disclosed about the issues with his children, their drug use, and his depression, the answer was consistently in the realm of, "He's one of us. We all have problems. He admitted it". The thing Bob Hawke and so many others thought would have brought him down was the very thing that won over a nation: Vulnerability!

Hawke led the Labor Party to victory for a total of three elections, in 1984, 1987 and 1990, thus making him the most successful Labor Leader in the history of Australia to date. Again: Vulnerability is power and it drives loyalty!

WHAT IF?

Just take a moment and consider someone you know who, at some point, despite everyone's counsel, decided to be accountable and tell the truth. I know if you think about it, you'll come up with someone. You figured if they did that, it would be their downfall—but it ended up being the very thing that elevated them.

So I say it again: Vulnerability is power and it drives loyalty!

POINTS TO PONDER From Chapter 9 ...

☀ Bob Hawke's story illustrates the importance of exposing the very things we have been trained to hide.

☀ Vulnerability is power and it is the driving force behind Fierce Loyalty.

Chapter Ten

Powerful—and Vulnerable

B rené Brown is a groundbreaking researcher in the field
of shame and vulnerability. In 2010, she was invited to
speak at a TED talk in her home town of Houston, Texas.
Despite her fears and reservations, she accepted the invitation, feeling like it was a hometown crowd and that the worst-
case scenario would be that if she sucked, only about 500 or
so people would get to see it.

In a later interview, Brené Brown tells us that six months later,
she received a congratulatory email from the Houston orga-
nizers telling her that the video of her talk was going to be
featured on the main TED website. As much as most speakers would be delighted at the news, Brené was terrified, and
wanted to find a way to hack into the system and delete the
video.

Not long after, the video went viral. As I write this, that video
on the power of vulnerability is the most viewed video on the
TED.com site, with more than five million hits.

The Power of Vulnerability

Brené's presentation was on The Power of Vulnerability, and I believe her work is at the forefront of influencing where we need to go as leaders. In the presentation, Brené speaks of her own hatred of vulnerability. Her plan was to understand how vulnerability works, and then she was going to, using her words, "outsmart it." She goes on to say that this clearly didn't turn out so well.

In that presentation, she also spoke about shame and worthiness, and I want to share some of her findings with you in order for you to understand the deep value of embracing vulnerability and to realize that it is your greatest source of power.

Brené speaks about how she roughly divided the people she interviewed into two main groups. One group consisted of people who really had a sense of worthiness, as well as a strong sense that they were loved and that they belonged. The other group consisted of folks who struggled with their worthiness, people who were always wondering if they were good enough.

She says that there was only one variable that separated the people who had a strong sense of love and belonging from the people who really struggled for it. That one variable was that the people who have a strong sense of love and belonging believe they're worthy of love and belonging. She says, "That's it." They believe they're worthy.

She goes on to speak about how the one thing that keeps us from feeling that deep sense of connection is our fear that we're not worthy of such a connection.

When speaking about herself, she said this was something that she felt like she needed to understand better both personally and professionally. So, as part of refining the research, she isolated all of the interviews where she saw worthiness, and just looked at those.

She wanted to understand: What do these people have in common? She goes on to say that she went back and pulled up all those interviews, their stories, and all their incidents to look for a theme. She wanted to know if there was a pattern.

The Courage to be Imperfect

What she found is the very thing we've been digging into here. What these people all had in common was a sense of courage. These folks very simply had the courage to be imperfect. They had the compassion to be kind to themselves first and then to others. These folks had a real sense of connection, and as a result, they were willing to let go of who they thought they should be in order to authentically be who they were. This is what you and I absolutely have to do for us to feel we have real connections in our personal and professional lives.

The other thing that these people had in common was something that completely surprised her. They all fully embraced vulnerability. What's more, they believed that what made them vulnerable was what made them beautiful.

Now, you may be feeling your skin crawl at the prospect of being vulnerable, and even saying something like, *Well it's easy for them, I'm just not built that way.* She says they didn't talk about vulnerability being comfortable, nor did they really talk about it being excruciating; they just talked about it being necessary. Did you get that? It may not be comfortable, but it sure as heck is necessary!

You are Worthy

Leadership is a tricky role to take on, and in all my years of working with a vast array of leaders from every walk of life, I can tell you that the vast majority feel like they are somehow fraudulent. They have told me on many occasions that even though they are in a position of leadership and power, they carry a secret fear of being found out. They doubt that they are fully qualified or educated enough, wise enough, old enough, young enough, successful enough, and a thousand other versions of "not good enough."

I share this with you because, as leaders, we need to learn from those wonderful people in Brené Brown's research, those people who not only felt that they had genuine connection, but also were worthy of it. They understand that vulnerability is necessary in order to get to that worthiness.

As excruciating as you may find the very idea of being vulnerable, I want to share with you how Brené Brown finished her presentation on the power of vulnerability. I want to give you this in her exact words, because we all need to embrace the power of vulnerability and courage, particularly in the face of fear, uncertainty, possible ridicule, and yes, even disconnection:

> "This is what I have found: to let ourselves be seen, deeply seen, vulnerably seen; to love with our whole hearts, even though there's no guarantee—and that's really hard, and

I can tell you as a parent, that's excruciatingly difficult.

"To practice gratitude and joy in those moments of terror, when we're wondering, 'Can I love you this much? Can I believe in this, this passionately? Can I be this fierce about this?'

"Just to be able to stop and, instead of catastrophizing what might happen, to say, 'I'm just so grateful, because to feel this vulnerable means I'm alive.'

"And the last, which I think is probably the most important, is to believe that we're enough. Because when we work from a place, I believe, that says, 'I'm enough,' then we stop screaming and start listening, we're kinder and gentler to the people around us, and we're kinder and gentler to ourselves."

Pairing Vulnerability and Leadership

For most of us, the mere idea of being vulnerable can be quite scary. However, pairing vulnerability and leadership can transform scary into a whole other level known as terrifying. After all, who among us has not been shamed in our vulnerability? Women leaders fear vulnerability because they have taken on the cultural conditioning that their rawness will be seen as hysteria. Men fear vulnerability because they too have taken on the cultural conditioning that to appear vulnerable would have them labeled as "wimps" or worse, "pussies."

That being said—highly effective, quality leaders are rare and always in demand, and that demand will only increase, while poor and even average leaders are a dime a dozen. If you intend to become a high quality leader and take leadership to the next level and depth, it will be necessary for you to challenge your cultural conditioning with regard to what a leader is and, for that matter, is not. You will need to examine, refine, and in some cases delete the thoughts and beliefs that do not facilitate your ability to best serve.

Leadership is Service

Leadership is about service. Vulnerable leadership is about serving from a place of compassion, caring, empathy, and vulnerability while holding fiercely healthy boundaries. This is not an I've read the book. I've got it kind of thing. This is a moment-to-moment balancing act that only those who are genuinely dedicated and committed to the highest possible level of leadership will have the courage to follow through on. Those who do have that level of dedication and commitment will lead the way, not only to what's possible in leadership, but also to what's possible for humanity as a whole.

FULL MONTY LEADERSHIP TIP

The vulnerable Leader constantly steps into the void even though s/he may have no real way of knowing what lies ahead.

The Vulnerable (Full Monty) Leader is an inspiration, because they are courageous, not just for themselves but for those they lead and for the vision they hold.

My Own Vulnerability

The first year we ran The Authentic Speakers Academy for Leadership was a very painful one for me. Over the years, many of my mentees had seen me give presentations and trainings in front of a wide variety of audiences, and on numerous occasions, they had told me that they wished I would share with them how to present with that level of passion, conviction, authenticity, and vulnerability.

Although I was flattered and honored, I told myself and them that I just didn't have the time. This, of course, was nonsense. As you and I both know, we make time for that which is genuinely important. The driving force throughout my speaking career has been to be of service to those who have influence—to influence the influencers—because that's how the world becomes a better place for all. Therefore, developing the curriculum for The Authentic Speakers Academy for Leadership took priority.

This was the first year, so I didn't have a reference point of exactly how what I wanted to do would turn out. In all honesty, as much as I knew with certainty that I could teach the program, I had no idea as to whether it would work or not—and I'll tell you up front, it didn't. At a business level, it was nothing short of a disaster. The program drained our bank account, our time, and most expensive of all, my emotional resources.

The first version of the program had a one-year curriculum with the goal of having a terrified novice complete looking and feeling like they had at least five, and hopefully ten, years of experience underneath their belt. For the experienced speaker, the goal was to take them out of performance mode and have them genuinely connect with their audience with such depth of rapport that it would build Fierce Loyalty and drive sales up by at least 200 percent.

As the program kicked off, I came together once a month with the twenty-four students. By the third month, a man who had many years before started out as a mentee and student of mine and had gone on to become a very close and dear friend stood up in class and said, *"Dov, I came here today to tender my resignation from the program. I don't believe our friendship can survive my being in the program, and I don't think this speaking thing is for me."*

Alan Lary was that student's name, and he is a man for whom I have an enormous amount of respect. He had figured highly in my decision to start the program. You see, Alan is a highly influential businessperson; he's a high-level soccer coach, he is a mentor, and he's someone who has consistently walked the talk of being a vulnerable leader. If he wanted to walk away, clearly something was wrong. As much as that old familiar audio/video loop of self-doubt could run in my mind directly after class, nonetheless, as he finished speaking, I continued to hold a vision of him (and for that matter, the entire class). I knew that vision was far bigger than the one he could hold for himself.—because, that's what a true mentor does.

As he finished speaking, I was disheartened and disappointed, but I would not let that get in the way. I instantly began to share a story with Alan and the class that I believed would illustrate what was going on. Thirty minutes later,

Alan stood up again and, with fierce conviction, said, *"I'm in, I'm committed!"*

Today, Alan Lary is an in-demand international speaker who mentors many powerful international business leaders in the fields of law, investment management, and accounting. However, as I said directly after I left that class, the audio/video loop of self-doubt began to play on every channel of my mind. To be completely honest, throughout the rest of that program there were many times where I just wanted to throw in the towel. However, I didn't, because I just knew this was all about something bigger than me or, for that matter, my very bruised and battered ego.

By the time the program was over, only five of the original group remained. Those five stayed the course because, as I had assured them, and it was true, I was holding a vision of them that was far bigger than the one they could hold for themselves. By the way, when you do this, you are doing what is truly required from you to be a great mentor. However, during the process, do not expect much thanks and, in fact, expect significant resistance. People, whether they know it or not—in fact, even when stating the opposite—are very attached to being pretty much where they are.

That was a tough year for me in many ways. It was my trial by fire as to whether I would actually walk my own talk at an even deeper level when it comes to being a vulnerable leader. Many times, I did the very thing that old school leaders would never do, or at least they would never admit to doing. I went home and cried, and what's more, I shared that I had done so.

As a leader, I was continually up against whether I could, in the face of constant resistance, keep the vision I was holding for them, all the while they themselves would constantly be abandoning it. Could I hold deep compassion for them and myself? Could I openly share what I was going through and at the same time hold to having the healthy boundaries needed to lead both personally and professionally? These and many more questions challenged me to be a better leader, and an authentic, vulnerable leader. And although I faltered many times, I stayed the course.

Today, the program has been significantly refined. Alan, the guy who said, "I'm not sure that speaking is for me," is now the head coach. We also have a team of other coaches and senior coaches, all of whom are graduates. Many of them have gone on to be international speakers. Each and every one of them would tell you that going through The Authentic Speaker Academy for Leadership was the toughest thing they have ever done and at the same time, the most rewarding thing they have ever done. Every one of them has had to step up into full-blown Authentic, Vulnerable Leadership, and as a result, they too are now leading and inspiring with vulnerability, caring, compassion, and fierce boundaries.

Vulnerable leadership is not easy, but I promise you, it is absolutely worth it!

POWERFUL AND VULNERABLE

POINTS TO PONDER From Chapter 10 ...

- 🔆 Brené Brown's research shows that vulnerability is your greatest source of power.

- 🔆 Vulnerability creates meaning and self-worth.

- 🔆 If you want to feel worthy, you must become vulnerable.

- 🔆 Leadership is service. You must learn how to serve from a place of compassion, caring, empathy, and vulnerability while holding fiercely healthy boundaries

- 🔆 Being a great mentor takes vulnerability.

Chapter Eleven

Courage is Not Optional

If you are going to be a vulnerable leader, then courage is more than a prerequisite. It's an absolute necessity!

Lessons From a Crab

It was going to be scorching. It was seven o'clock on a February morning and the sun was already hot on my back as I walked along City Beach, Western Australia. The tide was out and the sand had been pounded flat at the water's edge. Waves crashed on my right and the sun bounced off the sand in front of me like a spotlight searching for movement. A flock of small seabirds played at the shore, and then spotting their first meal of the day, they would suddenly and violently pierce the sand with their beaks.

I loved this walk. It was the perfect moving meditation. The smell and sound of the ocean were all-consuming, leaving my mind to simply marvel at the beauty that surrounded me.

Maybe you, like me, find that in such a moment you become a little more open, and a little of that most valuable gift bestowed upon to us in childhood springs forth—pure, unadulterated curiosity.

As I looked down at the sand, I saw a swarm of tiny little crabs running away from what must have seemed like a Godzilla-like figure moving towards them ... me. As they moved away, my eyes were drawn to another crab, a much larger crab. This crab was unusually large; its main shell was about the size of a grown man's spread out hand. This crab, however, was not running away. In fact, as I moved closed, it didn't even move a fraction of an inch.

As I got really close, I leaned down to grab the rear of the shell, away from the protruding claws. To my surprise, the shell had no real weight. What had once been a living animal was quite literally just a shell.

You have no doubt seen such a thing if you have spent time at the beach. I became curious: What happened to the crab that used to live inside this shell? Was it grabbed by a seabird and pried open to become an avian feast? Or did something else happen? That curious kid in me wanted to know.

Here's what I found out:

> In order for a crab or any crustacean to grow, it must periodically shed its old exoskeleton, a process called molting. The shell itself does grow, but that growth is minimal, hence the need for molting.

Mature crabs usually have to repeat this process about once a month, growing around 33 percent larger with each molt.

I could bore you with the hormonal details of how it all works, but let me skip to the highlights. Early in its molting cycle, the crab slowly begins to form a new soft shell underneath its existing hard shell.

In order to grow, the crab must face great discomfort. First the crab stops eating and, of course, during this process the crab is highly vulnerable to predators, including the two-legged variety!

As the process continues, the crab rapidly absorbs water through the old shell, which causes its tissues to swell. This in turn splits the old shell open across the back, between the lateral spines. Fracture planes in the claws split open to allow the new claws to be pulled through.

The crab, which has already been through what we can only presume to be a very uncomfortable process, now begins the slow, arduous process of backing out of its old shell. Then, with a last big push, the old outer shell is discarded like the one I found on the beach. The newly molted crab now pumps water into its tissues in order to inflate the shell to its new size. The new shell will be roughly one-third larger (33 percent) than the old shell. The new shell remains soft for around six hours after the molting of the old one in order for the new one to reach its full size.

What We Learned

As Authentic Vulnerable Full Monty Leaders we can learn a lot from our friend the crab. First, we learn that growth is inevitable. Imagine if the crab said, "Ah forget it, I'm not going to bother growing, it's just not convenient right now. Besides, the whole thing seems way too painful, I'm good the way I am." Yeah, that wouldn't work out too well.

Next, in order to facilitate the process of growth, the crab must stop eating. For us, that would mean for us to stop consuming whatever it is that feeds our ego's idea that we're okay and that we don't need to grow, particularly at this time.

Then the crab rapidly absorbs water through the old shell, which causes its tissues to swell. This in turn splits the old shell open. We as leaders must challenge ourselves to take in the information, knowledge, strategies, and feedback that will crack open the shell of our understanding. (Trust me, we all have such a shell.) Then, in order for the crab to become a third bigger, it must remain soft and vulnerable. Finally, the crab must repeat this potentially dangerous and vulnerable process about once a month.

FULL MONTY LEADERSHIP TIP

As Authentic Vulnerable Full Monty Leaders
we must be committed to continued growth,
no matter how uncomfortable it may be,
and no matter how safe it might feel
to stay where we are.

COURAGE IS NOT OPTIONAL

*The only true growth takes place
in the place we are most vulnerable.*

*Simply put, we cannot cling to being safe
while claiming that we are committed to growth.*

Change Requires Courage

The reason that courage is an absolute necessity in becoming an Authentic Vulnerable Full Monty Leader is that, in order to become such a leader, you have to face change and make changes. And change requires courage.

Meanwhile, for those who want traditional "leadership development," there are probably thousands of books to read and courses to take. But this book is for those who understand that not only has the economy changed, but the entire world of business has changed, and along with those changes has come a deep awakening that leadership at all levels must also change and evolve.

The good news is, some who had led using the old model will embrace the new style of leadership. They will do this because they understand that leadership is not just about having your followers do as you command, but rather having your followers flourish in an authentic environment of trust.

Business is now, more than ever, a process of relationship. However, as I've said many times before, those relationships must be transparent, authentic, and genuinely caring. This also means face-to-face business, not just with your customers, but with everyone in and on your team.

You Have to Let Them In

You have to let your colleagues, co-workers, and customers really see you, warts and all. In fact, the more you do so, the more they will be endeared to you, and in turn, the more fiercely they will endorse you as the "real thing."

In an article titled "10 Surprising Things That Benefit Our Brains That You Can Do Every Day,"[4] Belle Beth Cooper cites several fascinating experiments that changed the way she believed things work. One particular experiment once again validated the power of vulnerability when it comes to generating a bond.

Cooper sites the research done by psychologist Elliot Aronson into something known as The Pratfall Effect. During Aronson's test, he asked participants to listen to recordings of people answering a quiz. Certain recordings included the sound of the person knocking over a cup of coffee. When participants (those listening) were asked to rate the quizzers on likability, the coffee-spill group came out on top. Apparently, making mistakes actually makes us more likable, not less. This may, in fact, be the very reason why we tend to dislike people who seem perfect! Thanks to the research surrounding the Pratfall Effect, we know that making mistakes isn't the worst thing that could happen; in fact, it can work in your favor when it comes to generating a bond.

---

[4] Huffington Post (science), November 2013

The Time of the Vulnerable Leader

The days of leadership through intimidation are dimming, their dusk is falling, and the dark night will soon be upon them. The daybreak that is coming brings with it the light of Authentic Vulnerable Leadership, and it is already brightening the horizons of a world in desperate need of a new vision of leadership.

The time of the Vulnerable Leader is upon us.

POINTS TO PONDER From Chapter 11 ...

- ☼ Growth is inevitable. We either grow or we die.

- ☼ In order to facilitate the process of growth, we must stop believing that we don't need to grow.

- ☼ We must challenge ourselves to take in the information, knowledge, strategies, and feedback that will enable us to grow.

- ☼ In the process of growth, we become vulnerable.

- ☼ Courage is an absolute necessity, because growth requires change and change requires courage.

Chapter Twelve

The Hero's Journey

The great writer and visionary Joseph Campbell outlined the hero's journey in his classic work, *The Hero with a Thousand Faces.*

It seems to me that today's new leaders must enter that hero's journey. This journey is already changing the face of leadership and business. These new leaders will have to hold true to the path, while knowing that real treasure always is hidden in the darkest place. We must be courageous, because this dark place that we inherently fear we may never be able to come back from contains everything that will give our lives lasting meaning.

I know this to be true because I have journeyed there; I have faced the dragon that cannot be slain, but merely tamed. I have also had the honor of guiding many others on their own heroic journey.

But also know this: an Authentic Vulnerable Full Monty Leader is not without fear. However, such a leader's vision is the light that shines into the darkness, and it will always be greater than the fear.

As Joseph Campbell says, *"The cave you fear to enter holds the treasure you seek ..."*

Until you enter the cave, nothing will ever be enough! Do you have the courage to be an Authentic Vulnerable Full Monty Leader, to go in and claim that treasure on your own heroic journey?

Taming the Dragon

When we think of Leadership, it is rare to think of a leader as a real hero, particularly in contemporary times.

Unfortunately, the leaders we see today are often anti-heroes, men and women who lack the real characteristics—and character—that our world so desperately needs. While it's easy to be an anti-hero, becoming a hero in the true sense is a more challenging path.

But first, let's clear up any confusion about what we mean by "hero." I want to do this because what we're referring to is NOT the old-style corporate hero who gets flown in from some secret meeting on a private jet in order to bring XYZ Company back from the brink.

No, the kind of leadership hero we are speaking about here is the kind I spoke about a few pages ago, meaning a leader who has faced and tamed their own dragons.

When Joseph Campbell outlined the journey we must take if we are to become heroes, he could well have been speaking of the Authentic Vulnerable Full Monty Leader. This is because only those who have embraced the hero's journey will become the new face of leadership.

The Heroic Journey

Let me explain. In this magnificent piece of work, Campbell describes the many stages one must pass through on the "heroic journey." I believe it will give you a map of what it takes to become a vulnerable leader and the unexpected rewards it brings.

The would-be hero usually starts off as an ordinary human being, living in his or her ordinary world, playing the role they were given by those in authority. And even though they are in a role that by its very nature is inauthentic, this future hero/heroine often refuses to believe they are directed by anyone other than themselves.

But then, from what seems like out of nowhere, their ordinary world is shaken. Something catalytic, oftentimes tragic, happens to our future hero/heroine. This is a world-rocking, potentially perspective-shifting event that may come from some outside event or it may happen inside of them. However it comes, it's a major game-changer. This may be the final event in a series of such events (as it was for me), but it becomes "the call" to enter an adventure into the non-ordinary and vastly unfamiliar world, a world where this future heroine/hero will have to question everything they held as "real."

This is the call to a deep adventure that only those with the willingness to embrace the child-like and expansive trait of curiosity can take.

On this adventure, all preconceived certainty and all assumptions about how the world works will be brought into question. At this point, the traveler will either let go and accept that nothing will ever be the same, or they will get mired in fighting for beliefs that no longer hold true.

If our adventurer accepts the call to enter a new, strange reality, they must face a series of tasks and tests. At times, it will be important for our adventurer to face these tests alone. Other times, they may have a guide or a mentor. But whether alone or guided, they will have to face the challenges before them.

Before these trials are over, the adventurer will likely doubt their very sanity and certainly their capability. It is at this point that our traveler will sorely miss the familiar place they came from, and perhaps even temporarily forget the emptiness they felt there. They will long to go back to the ordinary world, the world they left behind, the world where they could blame others and play small.

At the most intense parts of the journey, the hero/heroine will be stripped naked of all their armor and stand in complete vulnerability. They will be forced to enter into some extremely dark and scary place and face some form of dragon or beast.

This beast will be a trickster that knows exactly how our adventurer has always thought and behaved and, as a result, it will always be one step ahead. This is now the dilemma of truth: will the adventurer cling to what they knew or look for new solutions? And so, the adventurer is forced to examine their most fundamental truths and beliefs about who they are, the purpose of their life, and the world they have lived in. It is in this moment of complete mental, emotional, even spiritual vulnerability that the adventurer will most likely perceive that their very life is threatened. This often elicits the most basic and raw emotions of our adventurer. They will likely have a breakdown that precedes the breakthrough needed to become the hero/heroine they are called to become.

At this point in the journey, the adventurer is usually offered a way out, a way to return to the familiar—a red pill or blue pill situation, if you will. Should the adventurer embrace vulnerability and not turn and run back to the familiar, but rather step into their courage in spite of being terrified, they will not only survive, but be gifted a great prize. It is at this point that our adventurer often discovers a deeply important and previously unknown knowledge and self-knowledge.

This is where everything changes, because now the adventurer must decide whether to return with the prize to the world/ reality from which they came. Returning will, in and of itself, be fraught with new challenges, all of which will give the hero/heroine the opportunity to deny what has happened and thus throw away the prize and reject the knowledge and self-knowledge they have been given.

However, should the heroine/hero be successful in returning to the ordinary world, the prize and self-knowledge may be used to improve the world from which she or he came.

What's important to realize is that a real "hero's journey" isn't undertaken to gain external accolades (even though these are most often a series of wonderful by-products), but rather for something far more rewarding: deep self-knowledge, meaningful contribution, and the real fulfillment that comes from creating a legacy.

Why Bother?

If you already have all that you want, if what you have many others envy, why would you or anyone in your position undertake such a journey?

The answer is simple. And yet, if you have even had an inkling of it, you will know the depth of its truth. Why would you take the heroic journey to become an authentically powerful, vulnerable leader? Because somewhere within you, you know that "everything" just isn't enough.

You know, deep inside, that you are meant for greater things, you are meant for the greatness that comes from not just great acts but rather from being open, compassionate, and caring in everyday situations. You know that you must enter onto the path that is the hero/heroine's journey in order for your life to have the deep meaning you want it to have. And you realize you must do this because, intuitively, you know that anything less will leave you empty without true purpose, without true fulfillment.

Everything you truly desire awaits you in that darkest of places.

Remember, an Authentic Vulnerable Full Monty Leader is not without fear. However, an Authentic Vulnerable Full Monty Leader's vision always needs to be greater than his or her fear.

Changing the Face of Business

The new leaders of the world—whether in business, community, nationally, or globally—are hearing the call to enter into the hero/heroine's journey, to embrace the power of becoming vulnerable leaders.

Those who have embraced this journey are already beginning to change the face of business.

As difficult as it may sometimes seem, these new leaders will hold true to the path, knowing that real treasure always is hidden in the darkest place. It is in this dark place, the place you inherently fear to go in case you never come back, that everything that will give your life and your organization meaning awaits.

Again, I know this to be true because I am a fellow traveler of this path.

My Journey

The hero's journey for me began on June 20, 1990. By this time, I had experienced many adventures. Many were envious of the life I'd lived. At thirty-two years old, I had traveled and lived in different parts of the world. I had met, studied, and hung out with world-class individuals. I had been on TV and radio and I had been written about in numerous newspapers and magazines. Life was good!

It was on that day, while engaging in the adrenaline sport of free climbing (climbing without ropes, or in my case, anything else) that my reality would be shifted in a way that would never allow me to see it the same again.

155

At somewhere around 120 feet (twelve stories), I reached for a rock that dislodged a bigger rock that hit me in the face, knocking me unconscious and sending me hurtling down to the sharp boulders below.

Five months and multiple reconstructive surgeries later, I looked reasonably fine, particularly if you had never met me before—but in truth, I was broken!

Everything I thought I knew about myself, the way the world works, and success had been shattered on those rocks. Although they were able to put my body back together, it was my heart, soul, and even my mind that needed fixing. What I can tell you is that the next year and half were even more excruciatingly painful than the previous five months had been.

Questions haunted my mind every single moment of both my waking and sleeping hours. From questions that were spawned from feeling like a victim—why me, what did I do to deserve this, to deeply philosophical questions about the meaning of life—especially the meaning of my life. I would wake up in the morning with deeply furrowed lines in my brow and cramps in my arms from sleeping in what my wife now calls the "bouncer pose": my arms tightly crossed over each other and a pissed-off look on my face.

During my recovery, I became reckless, using alcohol and drugs to subdue the emotional and mental pain that I would lie about, saying it was physical pain so that the doctor would write me another emotionally numbing prescription.

Eventually, I could no longer run from the pain, and I turned my focus inward. I began to look into those dark places. I began to see what I didn't want to see, including the fact that as much as a part of me wanted my old life back, it had felt somehow empty, like I, the real me wasn't in it, but rather some two-dimensional smiling version of myself playing the role of being successful.

It was during this time that I was introduced to someone I was told could really help me. Her name was Patricia Kitchener. Patricia was a very well-established therapist and a feminist who helped me understand what I had been doing to keep my relationship with women dysfunctional.

I chose to work with her because I was told that she was sharp as a whip and she would see through my shit, and call me on it. How right they were. I walked into her high-rise office space feeling pretty secure. I certainly wanted help in understanding what was happening for me, but I also knew I wasn't going to open up to someone I saw as a New Age flake. After the formal introduction and before she could say anything else, I somewhat arrogantly jumped in and said, "You better be really good, because I'm brilliant at covering up stuff, and if you don't catch me, I will run circles around you and me and I'll waste both our times, even though I don't want to do that. I want, no, I need your help." (As I said earlier in this book, people will fight to hold onto that which they claim to dislike.)

Patricia looked at me with warm certainty, and said with a big smile, "Oh, I'm really good. I'm already on to you, and I will not be letting you pull any of your shit here—including trying to take control of our sessions." In that moment, I knew I'd found someone I could trust and respect.

The next year or so, Patricia assisted me in looking into as many dark places as we could find and many more I didn't want to look into. In fact, I can clearly remember saying to Patricia things like, "Yeah, we don't need to go there. I've already done a lot of work on that." I wasn't lying; I had done many years of self-discovery before I fell, but the fall had broken open new layers of the walls I had used to protect myself.

It didn't take me long to realize Humpty Dumpty had not only fallen and couldn't be put back together again, but more importantly, I didn't want to try and put myself back together the way I had been. It was time for me to rediscover what had been lost and make that my driving force.

For me, it was all about starting over. I knew that as a boy I'd been open-hearted and highly creative with a fiercely curious mind. I also knew that I had been ridiculed for being so. It didn't take long before I was able to pull off looking like I was tough, even though inside I never felt that was who I was. I had grown up in an environment where "real men" never showed their feelings, with the exception of being horny, hungry, or angry (those were apparently acceptable); any other feeling would just make me "vulnerable," and no one wanted to be that. And so, like every man I knew, I hid my true feelings from everyone, especially myself.

As I did the work with Patricia, the macho image I had held for so long got cracked open just as surely as my head did on those rocks.

I won't lie to you. I had sessions where emotions would wash over me like a tsunami, and I'd feel like I was going to drown.

But with time, those tsunamis would become welcome sun showers on a hot August night. And instead of leaving devastation in their wake, they left fertile ground in which I could plant the seeds of my future.

As I healed, I returned to my vocation; however, even though from the outside it may have looked the same, from the inside, everything was different. If I were going to lead again, I would have to raise the level and quality of my leadership. I would have to lead from a place of embracing the power of my own vulnerability. I would have to do so with compassion, caring, and the willingness to hold fiercely healthy boundaries with myself and others, too.

I do admit that I was afraid to be vulnerable, but I knew that if I didn't model vulnerability, those I mentored would continue to be held prisoner by their pain, just as surely as I had been by mine. Repressing the pain had limited my ability to lead not only others but, more importantly, myself. That repression had limited my ability to experience the full spectrum of life, and I was no longer going to be part of the problem, so I chose to be a demonstration of the solution.

I took myself off the pedestal and openly shared that I was/am no better and no worse than anyone I mentor. While at the same time, I was fierce about the fact that people can get real with me or they can get out. I was no longer willing to be "nice" (Neurotically Insecure Controlling my Emotions). I was going to stand in my truth and call bullshit where I saw it.

And while defending my boundaries, I would be there for my clients in a way that would be totally unfamiliar. That meant I would hold a vision for them of them owning their greatness and being whole in doing so, and I would hold it from a place of deep empathy, compassion, caring, and love.

As you can imagine, this scares the crap out of some folks. Some saw my certainty and clarity of purpose as arrogant, while others just recoiled back into their self-protecting egoic shells, all the while telling me that if they really stepped up, they would hurt too many people and they just couldn't do that. I respect that choice and would tell them, with that same level of clarity, that I could not serve them.

I began telling my story and not censoring out the things that wouldn't make me look so good. I even began to explain that, while it appeared that I fell off a mountainside and landed on my head, in truth, what really happened was that I had fallen off a self-imposed pedestal and landed on my ego.

Only when I started to open up did I attract into my life the woman I had been waiting for, a woman I was just not ready for until that time. Through embracing the power of vulnerability, I was finding more joy in my work and in my life in general.

THE HERO'S JOURNEY

*Real leaders face challenges
and even embrace them.*

*Just telling myself and others that
I wore emotional armor
because I was a warrior,
didn't make me a warrior.
Not having the courage
to look into the dark places
and face the dragon at every turn
made me a coward.*

*I have discovered that stripping off the armor
and being emotionally naked
is the only way to live in the full spectrum
of this beautiful thing called life.*

POINTS TO PONDER From Chapter 12 ...

🔆 The cave you fear to enter holds the treasure you seek.

🔆 The Hero's Journey is a map of what it takes to become a vulnerable leader and the unexpected rewards it brings.

🔆 A real "hero's journey" is undertaken to gain deep self-knowledge, meaningful contribution, and the real fulfillment that comes from creating a legacy.

🔆 You will know that you must enter the hero/heroine's journey in order for your life to have the deep meaning, you want it to have, when you get a sense that everything will never be enough.

Chapter Thirteen

Identity and Loyalty

One of the central themes of this book has been that business and leadership must become centered in healthy, empowering relationships.

"Relationships are difficult because people are complicated," is something I hear from leaders all the time. As someone who was originally trained as a psychotherapist, and after almost thirty years in the personal development seminar field, I can tell you that relationships are difficult and yes, people seem complicated, but there are certain subconscious, fundamental drivers that are pushing and pulling them, often in directions that they wouldn't consciously choose to go. When you recognize those drivers, people are far easier to understand and relationships are a heck of a lot more satisfying for all concerned.

The Desire to Belong

One of the most basic drivers is that of survival. People will do some pretty wild stuff when they feel that their survival is threatened, but that's another book. However, once our basic survival is covered, one of the greatest drivers of human beings is the desire to belong; we all want to be part of something.

This, however, is a bit of a dichotomy, because the desire to belong often falls into conflict with an equally deep desire to know who we are.

For some folks, knowing who they are is easy—at least for a while. Such a person will tell themselves, and will feel it reinforced by the environment, that who they are is the group that they are in some way associated with. For example, we may say we are a Thompson or a Smith, meaning that we claim "we are" the family we are born into. For others it's a religion or an ethnicity. For others, it's an ideal: I'm a Republican, a Democrat, a feminist, a skeptic, a pragmatist, an optimist etc. You get the picture.

The reason I said knowing who we are is easy for some "for a while" is because they get to belong by saying who they are is the group with which they have associated themselves. However, there is a natural evolution to the question that, at some point, will have us step back from ourselves and ask: If who I am is not the group, then who am I?

Identity Crisis

We tend to call this an identity crisis, and it's at that moment when the group will likely run in and start plugging all the holes you've been poking in your identity by telling you all the reasons you are one of them. If, however, you keep going, the group will in all likelihood turn its back on you and treat you like a pimple on the nose of their collective identity. This, of course, can feel very painful, because it's what is called a "values" pain, meaning there is a clash between those two driving forces: the desire to know who you are and the desire to belong.

Where you go from there deeply depends on your level of self-worth, inner strength, and support system for exploration. What I can tell you with absolute certainty is that very few people make it through to the other side without a support system. By the way, if you think you're the exception to the rule, you're probably not, and that's the thinking that will have you conforming and being filled with resentment for having done so.

The Bond in the Beginning
In the beginning there was the bond! Before we even enter into this world, we are deeply reliant on others. While you are in the womb, your very survival depends on another. And whether you see yourself as a needy person or a lone wolf, this primal conditioning runs as a driving theme in all of us. That being said, it is far more obvious in some than it is in others. Some who characterize themselves as lone wolves hide it well, but I promise you, it's there. And if we are not paying attention, it will come rolling in like a coastal fog in the night. You don't see it coming, but just in the moment of needing absolute clarity, it will obscure your view and have you mentally or emotionally landlocked to the familiar.

Survival of the Fittest?
Charles Darwin is often credited with coining the phrase "the survival of the fittest." However, neither the quote nor its meaning is correct, and this has had immeasurable impact on business, leadership, and our global society in general.

What Darwin actually wrote was "that traits which allow individual organisms to reproduce successfully will appear disproportionately in successive generations." Darwin never said it's "the survival of the fittest." That was created by a gentleman by the name of Herbert Spencer. Darwin did later use Spencer's term. However, anthropologists now agree that what Darwin meant by using the term "fittest" was *the one best suited for the immediate environment*. Sadly, we have en masse, and particularly in the world of business, misconstrued that the phrase means "the best will win" and used this understanding to be involved in and to justify highly hostile and often vicious competition.

For the more than one hundred years since Darwin wrote *The Origin of Species*, this misunderstood quote has shaped our world view and had us buy into the idea that, when it comes down to it, we are all isolated beings competing for survival by whatever means.

What's even worse, in believing this misconception, we have developed the idea that life is random, purposeless, solitary, and of course, predatory. It has given us the paradigm that the universe is a huge machine and man is a survival machine, and we have fashioned our world from within this paradigm. However, the latest research and evidence emerging from the world of quantum physics—and yes, even biology—tells us a radically different story.

Bestselling author of *The Bond*, Lynne McTaggart, shares that the latest science is clear: We are not naturally in competition, but rather, we exist in a dynamic relationship of connection and constant influence. Cooperation and even sacrifice are intrinsic to the biological makeup not just of us, but of all living things.

Shocking as it may be to those who have lived their lives believing that they, particularly as leaders, must keep their distance and be the lone wolf, there have been surprising new discoveries in biology and the social sciences that have profoundly altered our world view, particularly that of the relationship between living things and their environment.

What has become vividly clear is that, between the smallest particles of our being, our bodies, and our environment . . . and between ourselves and all of the people within our sphere of influence . . . in fact, between every member of every societal cluster, there is a bond.

The Bond that Binds

Before you write this off as some kind of New Age woo-woo stuff, let me walk you through exactly what I mean. The most contemporary scientific research is now showing that there is a connection so integral and profound that, despite our ego-based idea that we are alone, there is no longer a clear demarcation between where one thing ends and another begins. Science now clearly says that the world, for all intents and purposes, operates not through or because of the activity of the individual or even individual things, but rather in the connection between them. There is a bond that binds us all.

Even though we have desperately clung onto the idea that our survival depends on our willingness to be isolated and even ruthless if needed, what's being made clear is that the most vital aspect of life is not in our ability to stay isolated, but rather in our ability to recognize our connection to others. What McTaggart clearly outlines is that, in every way, individual things live life inextricably attached and bonded to an "other."

She goes on to show that, whether it's at the subatomic level or that of being a fully formed living being, it is the relationship between things that is the foundation of not only the potential for survival, but our ability to thrive in any given environment. She goes on to show that there is an inseparable, irreducible bond between all things. She has us see that honoring this connection, this bond, is what actually holds the key to life for any organism, from the subatomic particles level all the way to large-scale societies, and honoring that bond is the key to our viable future.

These discoveries not only hold vast implications about how we choose to define ourselves, they also hold vast implications about how we may want to choose to live our lives. They give us the opportunity to reassess the two things we spoke about earlier: meaning and purpose.

The research suggests that we have falsely created societal structures that are so invested and embedded in competition—and with them, the potential for an individual to dominate—that the structures we create actually run totally counter to our most fundamental being and the greatest opportunity for us all to flourish. As we move forward, understanding that our strength is in our bond turns the old model of leadership completely on its head, while at the same time presenting you, the leader, a clear way to move forward and change the face of leadership as we have known it.

Lessons From the Delivery Room

I have no idea whether you are a parent or not, but if you are, and particularly if you have children who are now grown up or at least young adults, what I am about to share with you will be glaringly obvious once I point it out. For those who are not parents, I know you will have observed this in family members or even the children of friends. However, no matter what your parental situation is, if you are really honest, you will certainly see yourself in this.

Picture this; you are in the delivery room, the lights are bright, the tension is high, and you are either crushing your partner's hand or they are crushing yours as that final push has another human life enter the world. Suddenly all the screaming pain, sweat, and anxiety were worth it; you are part of what feels like a miraculous experience, that of creating a child.

Taking that child in your arms, you instantly fall in love. There in your arms is an amazing little being whose potential is so vast, you can't even fathom it. In all likelihood, somewhere in there will be a moment (or longer) of feeling complete. The words may even slip from your lips as you look at the baby and then your partner and say, "Now we are complete. Now we are a family."

As time goes by you take your baby home and each day you look at it with wonder and awe and fall ever more deeply in love with this eating, sleeping, crying, and—let's face it—shitting machine. Why? Well among other things, it's because we human beings are pack animals; we want to bond and belong and our neurology and biology are designed to support that. As a result, every time we hold our child or have some kind of bonding moment, our brain releases a neurochemical cascade from the mood and appetite center of our brain, which is called the hypothalamus. The hypothalamus works in concert with other parts of the endocrine system and an extremely powerful cocktail of hormones are released including, among others, vasopressin, and most powerful of all, oxytocin.

The research suggests that when we hug or kiss a loved one (not just a baby), oxytocin levels are increased. This hormone originates in the pituitary gland and acts as a neurotransmitter in the brain for other hormones. The research has shown that oxytocin is the hormone that plays a powerful role in pair bonding, meaning it's a major player in determining whom we fall in love with. This hormone is stimulated to some degree whenever we are with a loved one. However, the largest doses are flooded into the system during the birthing process, breast-feeding, and sex. This hormone may be a major contributing factor as to why you don't throw that eating, sleeping, crying, and shitting machine called a baby out of the window when you haven't had a complete night's sleep in months.

It should also be noted that we are in the early stages of understanding this hormone. However, even though scientists currently know oxytocin is released during the events just mentioned, it is also suspected to be released when we are in deep discussions or when we are feeling "gotten" (and that is of vital importance for leaders who are looking to generate Fierce Loyalty in our teams). In other words, we can have a deeply bonding experience without physical touch when someone we are with is responding to us in a genuinely empathetic manner. The more recent research has shown other roles for the hormone oxytocin. For instance, oxytocin levels are high under stressful conditions, such as combat. This helps explain the bond that takes place between brothers in arms. But here's where it gets very interesting: oxytocin has been shown to be highly linked to influencing trust and social attachment.

Stay with me here if you really want to know what generates Fierce Loyalty.

Becoming an Individual

Child psychologists tell us that for the first months of a baby's life, a child has no sense of itself as being separate from everything that surrounds it. As the child gets a little older, we begin to correct its behavior and start teaching our child the difference between right and wrong, essentially passing on our beliefs and values.

It is during this time that a child's mind is wide open. Research indicates that we learn more between the ages of zero through four than we do the rest of our lives. At this point in our development, we turn nothing away, allowing every limited idea in as if it were an absolute truth given to us by a heavenly being.

However, once we hit somewhere between eighteen months and two years old, depending on the child, we do begin to develop a sense of ourselves. We get, at least at some level, that mom, dad, and everything else is not who we are. At this point, we want to feel safe enough to explore our world both physically and psychologically. This is also the time when most healthy children will find a new favorite word: No! What is it with this emphatic and somewhat automatic "no"? Well, you'll be glad to know it's not personal. That no is the beginning of a very healthy and important stage of development called Individuation.

I'm Not You
Individuation is simply: "I'm not you." It's the testing and expanding of the psychological boundaries.

At this first step in the process, some parents will shut that kid down so fast they won't know what hit them, and if that's repeated often enough, the child will learn that the only safe thing to do is repress their own personality and comply.

Other parents (and they are rare) will allow, even support these physical and psychological explorations, thus giving that child a healthy sense of self and a deeper sense of safety in the world.

I Don't Believe What You Believe
By the time the child reaches its teens, it has reached the second stage of individuation: "I don't believe what you believe."

If the repression was fierce enough in the first stage, a kid may skirt right through adolescence without ever breaking the rules or doing anything to rebel. As much as the parents of such a child may feel "we raised our child right," this is not a good thing. If the child is healthy, they will go out and break rules—not just the parents' rules, but in all likelihood, also the rules of society.

At this point, some parents will not only shut that kid down, they may further indoctrinate the teen with how they are not lovable to either the parent and or society when they behave in a certain manner. If this kind of feedback is repeated often enough, that adolescent may decide that the only safe thing to do is comply.

Other parents (and again they are rare) will allow, even support these physical and psychological explorations by setting up healthy boundaries through co-designed agreements and consequences with their teen-aged child. This gives the adolescent a healthy sense of self (autonomy) and a deeper sense that it is safe to explore rather than just conform.

I Am NOT Who I Believed I Was

There is a third stage of individuation: "I'm not who or what I have believed I was." Often this is referred to as "midlife crisis." In this stage, there is a deepening dissatisfaction with our own lives. The argument may be mired in the thick mud of guilt. "A person may repress themselves and tell themselves to be more grateful, but that nagging feeling just won't go away. At this point, some folks hit the touchstone of the familiar, doing more of what they have always done—like buying expensive toys or working even harder.

For other people, they figure that this lack of satisfaction is because of their spouse and or family. These folks may find themselves entangled in sordid affairs. For others, the idea of walking away is too much and they are too emotionally invested in "being their image," so that to cope, they become addicted to something (which could be a substance or just as easily a behavior) that will waylay the desire to run away like their hair is on fire.

In each of these stages, we are torn between the two basic human desires: that of bonding and belonging versus that of individuating from the very group we are bonded with. I've shared this knowledge with you because it is vital for you to understand when it comes to generating Fierce Loyalty in your people.

Generating Fierce Loyalty

Putting it as plainly as possible: Your people will be Fiercely Loyal if they are given a safe environment in which they can express their individuality, and if they feel a sense of autonomy. This is best done in an environment of like-minded individuals with whom they have intimacy (preferably non-sexual). These individuals are a collective group who support each other in developing mastery in their own area, in what I will refer to as personal leadership. There is a common, driving purpose and bond to each other and to the organization that comes from doing meaningful work.

You will note that nowhere in there was salary a bonding factor. Because, as stated in an earlier chapter, money only matters until it doesn't, while feeling that we belong and that it is safe for us to bond are unchanging. Human beings need to know that they matter and we are hard-wired to bond and we want that bond no matter how hardened we may seem. Therefore, if an employer can create an environment where bonding, belonging, meaning, and purpose are nurtured, there really is very little reason to leave!

If we are going to turn our organizations into ones that foster Fierce Loyalty, we must develop a corporate culture based on creating leaders rather than followers. Please understand that I get it, not everyone wants to lead others. However, everyone in your organization needs to be encouraged to lead themselves. As you well know, there is little that's more frustrating and time-wasting than an employee who is always waiting to be told what to do next. This is fine in the beginning; however, if it continues, instead of having an asset, you have someone who drains resources and—to not put not too fine a point on it—you need to get rid of them!

Your Leadership Style

At this point, it is important to stop and be really honest with yourself about your own leadership style. So right now, take a moment and just ask yourself: Are you genuinely developing leaders or facilitating your people to be followers?

If you answered "developing leaders," congratulations. However, are you sure about that?

As someone with my ear to the ground regarding the world of leadership, I hear all kinds of chatter about leadership and leadership development. Sadly, when I dig a little deeper, that chatter and even the trainings are not really about leadership development, but rather about making sure that you know how to get others to follow the leader.

Having read this far, you now have an understanding that one of the drivers that will keep your people loyal is a sense of autonomy.

FULL MONTY LEADERSHIP TIP

*Therefore, I put it to you that
your organization needs to be training
people in the skills that
are required not just to make others follow,
but in the skills required to lead leaders.*

Peer Level

Here's why this is important: your people will rise or fall to the level of their peers, which is often the lowest common denominator. What this means is that people end up being "led" by example, and if the example is that of a weak leader, then that weak leader is not only failing those s/he is leading, but also his or her peer leaders. As a result, any leader you have on board who is a true leader will simply walk away and at least quietly see you as weak. However, should a strong leader stay in an environment of weak leaders, there's a pretty good chance that they will become as weak and inept as their peers.

When we treat our leaders as followers, we are telling them that there is no room for that great bonding agent—autonomy. Therefore, the transparency and accountability that are vital in today's business world get strangled out.

Consequences vs. Punishments

Remember earlier when we talked about the rare parents who will allow and even support a child's physical and psychological explorations by setting up healthy boundaries through co-designed agreements and consequences?

176

Authentic leadership development is a very similar process. Your leaders need to know and agree on the boundaries of their power and autonomy. There is a crucial need to sit with them and have them design consequences (which you can negotiate to your mutual satisfaction) for not having kept agreements, or having broken any agreed-upon boundary. Again, this is vital because, as a leader developing and leading other leaders, you never want to treat them like children. This was the model for old-school dictatorial leadership, and it certainly got people to comply, but it never got them to give their best.

This model of conscious agreements and agreed-upon consequences then becomes a model your leaders use with those they lead. I will warn you, though, if you let an agreement get broken and you do not hold your people to the consequence, this will come down on you like a house of cards.

A Personal Example

Let me give you a personal example. When Michael, my son, was sixteen (age sixteen equals stage two of individuation), we sat down to design a set of agreements and consequences around behaviors, attitudes, and chores. We did this because, even though I can be a fairly intimidating force, I have no desire to intimidate anyone. Even then, Michael was a bright young man and I wanted to empower him to be a leader in his own life. We worked on what we were doing for about an hour and reached the end point where Michael wrote down each specific agreement and the specific, correlating consequence. Having completed them, I asked him how he felt about them and he said, "Good." Once again, I reiterated that I had no desire to punish him for anything, but rather wanted to encourage him to be a leader and hold himself both responsible and consequential. He said he understood, we hugged, and we went on with whatever we were doing.

For the next few weeks, Michael was pretty good in that he kept most of his agreements. There was an occasion where he had not done one of his minor chores within the allotted time frame and he asked me if we could let it slide, as it was "no big deal." I simply said, "It's not up to me. These are your agreements and your consequences." At that point, he quietly got up and did whatever it was that he'd agreed to as a consequence.

This was all working great until something major happened. You don't need to know the details except that we had already covered it in our original discussion. Before I go any further, you should know that Michael was pretty normal in that he did some "rebellious stuff" as part of his individuation, but overall, he was a really good kid.

Anyway, he did this certain thing, and the consequence was very severe for him: he could not go to the gym for five back-to-back days. Now I know that for some people, that consequence would seem like a gift, but not for Michael. You see, Michael was a fanatical body builder, and not working out for five days equated to torture. However, that was the agreed-upon consequence. By the end of the second day, I could tell he was climbing the walls. On the third day, as I walked in the door, my wife said, "Michael wants to talk to you." She whispered that he and been really good, doing lots of extra chores without being asked, and that he had asked her what he must now ask me because she had told him, "Your agreement is with Dov, not me, and that's who you need to speak to."

I walked into the living room and gave Michael the usual hug and said, "Your mom says you want to talk to me." He replied, somewhat sheepishly with a low volume, "Yeah."

"Okay, let's go in your room."

When we got there, we sat on the bed and I looked him in the eye while he told me all the good stuff he had been doing, above and beyond his chore list. I listened and did not interrupt. Then he said, "Well, this is the third night. Do you think I could go to the gym?"

Like I said, Michael was a good kid, and in truth, every part of me wanted to say yes—but I fought the urge and just let myself sit in the discomfort of it all. Then I asked Michael a few questions. "Whenever I've said I'll do something for you, do I do it, even if it's inconvenient for me?"

Michael looked a little puzzled when he said, "Yeah, I guess."

I went on. "Have I always kept my word with you?"

Again, Michael replied in the affirmative.
"Do you trust me, Michael?"

Once again, "Yes" was his response.

"Well, I want to be able to trust you and I want you to keep trusting me, and that's why I am going to be a man of my word and I'm going to ask you to be the same."

Michael looked at me and forced a smile. I told him I loved him and that I was proud of him. I gave him a hug and left his room. Michael went ahead and missed five back-to-back workouts without complaining.

Now at this point, you may be thinking that's all very interesting, but my team are not sixteen year olds. However, working with a team that you are encouraging to be authentic and accountable leaders is no different: you must hold them as leaders and support their owning their power and responsibilities, even when it would be easier for them to abdicate power to you. I promise you, this is a powerful loyalty builder because you are refusing to let go of your vision of them as leaders.

In the Authentic Speakers Academy for Leadership, we have everyone agree to live by a certain set of principles and codes of conduct. These principles and codes of conduct are designed to have the mentees hold themselves to being leaders in everything they do, day in and day out throughout the training.

On Day One of the eight-month training, they choose and set significant consequences that they'll hold themselves to for the entire program. Needless to say, depending on the individual and the consequences they've set, we've had people get into much better cardio shape due to week-long consequences that involved 5 a.m. workouts. Others have given many thousands of dollars to a range of charities, and still others have suffered many wilder and sometimes wacky consequences.

IDENTITY AND LOYALTY

POINTS TO PONDER From Chapter 13 ...

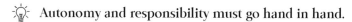 Autonomy and responsibility must go hand in hand.

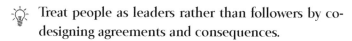 Treat people as leaders rather than followers by co-designing agreements and consequences.

☀ As a Full Monty Leader who wants Fiercely Loyal talent, you must hold your people to their agreements and consequences if you want to instill deep trust.

Chapter Fourteen

The Power of Storytelling

We have all heard the saying "no man (or woman) is an island" and, although we may intellectually understand that, far too many folks operate as if they are alone in the ocean.

Off the Island

Stories are our way to get off that psychological island, and what's more, they are a way off the island of our own bias. In the words of storyteller and novelist Elif Shafak:

> "We tend to form clusters based on similarity, and then we produce stereotypes based on clusters of other people. In my opinion, one way of transcending these cultural ghettos is through the art of storytelling. Stories cannot not demolish frontiers, but they can punch holes in our mental walls, and through those holes we can get a glimpse of the other and sometimes even like what we see."

Full Monty storytelling is a powerful tool that allows us to not only see something we may never have previously imagined, but also to feel something we may never had known existed within us. Storytelling gives us ways to peer into a world where we may have seen only adversaries and, instead, see reflections of ourselves in a facet of another. Full Monty storytelling takes down the walls of corporate silos faster than demolition dynamite embedded in an old stadium.

Storytelling has always had the power to relay messages and history and also has been the most powerful medium for moving the hearts, minds, feet, and the bank accounts of listeners in the direction the storyteller determines.

Attachment, Meaning, and Loyalty

"We are family, and we stick by each other, no matter what."

"Blood is thicker than water."

These sayings are ones we are all familiar with; they imply that "family is first" and that when the chips are down, there's no greater bond than that of family.

For most people, the bond to family is a very strong one. However, most of us also have had some kind of extraordinary experience with someone who was not a family member, an experience that somehow deeply bonded us. Oftentimes, such an experience is so profound that it bonds us in such a way that we may now jokingly refer to each other as siblings or at least "family."

For example, the soldier who serves side-by-side with his or her comrade in arms may experience this kind of bonding. Two (or more) climbers on a particularly difficult climb—a climb where you literally have to put your life in the hands of another—may very well create such a profound bonding experience.

Such a bond is not exclusively created in "life or death" situations, but it is always formed in common experience that, without doubt, includes a milieu of mutual vulnerability.

Such a bond can be found between teammates, college buddies, even sisters of a sorority. Let me ask you: how did you meet your best friend? For some of you, that friendship grew over time. For others, it was instantaneous.

Let's go back to family for a moment. As much as we have all somehow gotten the message that "family is first," "we are family," and "blood is thicker than water," even in family we are not equally bonded. If you grew up in a large family with many siblings or if you had a large extended family, you know that, in all likelihood, you have a much stronger bond with certain individuals than you do with the others. In fact, outside of the family conditioning, your relationships with outsiders (friends) are in all likelihood no different than those inside your family: you are closer to one or a few people than you are to the others.

How Bonds are Formed

How are these bonds formed, and what can they tell us about having our people and our teams become Fiercely Loyal, not just with each other, but with the organization?

Bonding and knowing how to attach are vital to our emotional/mental development and to our very survival. In fact, we know that a person who, for whatever reason, in early childhood had the experience of either not attaching to a primary caregiver or having that bond broken very early, will often have a hard time bonding and attaching throughout the rest of their lives. In many cases, such individuals will suffer from at least low-level feelings of isolation and mistrust of others. Of course, at the extreme end of the spectrum, such a person can suffer from sociopathic tendencies.

In a reasonably emotionally healthy individual, there is (and should be) at least a mild dose of skepticism before any real bonding and trust is built. We say that we want to take people at face value, but in truth, we want and need them to show that they are consistent in order for us to trust them and potentially bond with them.

Obviously, we go through our foundational bonding experiences very early on in life. As infants, we become attached to the individual or individuals who are sensitive and responsive to our needs. This is particularly true in the social interactions we have during the first two years of our lives. It is our awareness of how people respond to our needs that is known as "sensitive responsiveness."

Think about when you fell in love. You probably felt that one of the things you loved about that person was that they seemed to know what you needed, maybe even before you did. That's the "sensitive responsiveness" that generates attachment and deep bonding.

A Secure Base

When an infant begins to crawl and walk, they begin to explore a world that is bigger than the primary caregivers' field of view. However, should that infant leave the view of the primary caregiver for too long, then they will likely feel a degree of anxiety, depending on how far away the infant perceives the primary caregiver to be and the depth of the bond with the primary caregiver. Therefore, infants use attachment figures (primary caregivers) as a secure base to explore the world from and a safe place to return to.

The way the caregiver responds to a developing child will lead to the development and patterns of attachment in that individual. These formative experiences of bonding and having needs met (or not) will in turn lead to the emotional/mental working model this person has for bonding. This, in turn, becomes both the map of where they can go and the lenses through which this individual sees the world. As a result, this guides the individual's thoughts, emotions, perceptions, beliefs, and expectations in all later relationships.

The concept of the "secure base" comes out of research done by developmental psychologist Mary Ainsworth, which came into fruition back in the 1960s and '70s and has led to great advances by other truly brilliant psychologists. In truth, "attachment" and "attachment styles" is a vast and fascinating subject. However, for reasons of expedience, I will not be going any deeper into it here. What you need to know is that we all need to attach and bond, and that knowledge is vitally important information for you as a leader looking to generate Fierce Loyalty.

What it Means

What all this means to you is that, if you want to generate Fierce Loyalty in your team, you have to find ways to bond your team to each other and the organization in a way that gives them the emotional experience of a "secure base."

Throughout our lives, we continue to form bonds with others. Earlier in this book, I spoke of "The Bond" and how we are bonded at birth and that we have a whole neuro and biological system set up to make sure we do bond. However, we continue to bond throughout our lives. For instance, you may not have met your best friend until you were in college or even in your twenties or thirties, so obviously, bonding is not limited to our formative years (even if the model of how you bond is).

Bonding and the power of generating a bond cannot be overstated when it comes to knowing how to generate Fierce Loyalty in your leadership teams and your overall organization. Knowing how to catalyze such a bond means that, if your competitors were to offer your top talent a "better deal," they would barely even consider it. As I am sure you can already see, creating a secure base bond has enormous value.

A Practical Exercise

So let's start a follow-along exercise:

Think back to the time when you met someone you are now very close to, someone you feel you have a strong bond with. If I ask you to pinpoint the moment when you knew there was a real connection with that person, you may or may not be able to think of that instant. However, if I ask you to now go back and think of some of the moments when you shared something important with each other, fairly quickly you will have a flood of memories wash over your mind. These memories will be moments when you felt like "you were on the same page"—"on the same team"—"pulling together"—or using the term I spoke of earlier in the book, a moment of being "gotten."

Now, as you think back and remember any one of those memories that you shared with this person, I want you to think about how many times you have told that story. Now some of you will say that this is a story you don't tell, and if that's the case, then I would suggest that whenever you and this person get together, somehow or in some way, that story surfaces. On the other hand, if it's a more public story, depending on how significant it is, it's likely to be a story you tell all the time.

Stories Cement Bonds

So, why do we retell stories, and what's that got to do with having your team become Fiercely Loyal? Brace yourself. We retell stories because, each time we retell the story, we re-cement the bond implied in the story.

What's more, if we tell the story in a compelling enough way, others will take that story and retell it. Why? Because if a story is told well, it engages the listener. In other words, they will insert themselves into your story in some way and, consciously or unconsciously, it somehow becomes their own story, and that certainly re-cements the bond.

Our Story

My wife and I met on a blind date through a friend of mine who somehow decided that it was his mission in life to set me up. Sadly, he was always trying to set me up with women he found attractive. (Let's just say we have very different tastes.) After a couple of these fix-ups, I told him to back off, and he did ... for a while. About a month had gone by when suddenly he called me and he was all excited because, as he said, "I've got one for you."

I immediately thought, *Oh no, not another "Barbie blonde."* (I am attracted to dark-skinned, exotic-looking women, and he likes more Barbie-like women.)

So I said, "No thanks, mate. There's nothing wrong with what you like. However, you and I do not have the same taste in women."

He assured me that this lady was curvy and exotic. Okay, he had my attention.

Apparently, he called her up and told her that he had someone he thought she should meet. She, being an empowered, modern woman, said okay, and the next day she called me. We had three calls and, over the phone, we hit it off right away. She told me that she was going away to Mexico for a week and we decided that we should meet in person upon her return.

The day before the reveal (remember, we had no idea what either of us looked like and this was pre-Facebook), we spoke again on the phone. I guess it hit her that, despite the fact that we had been getting along fabulously on the phone, she had no idea about any of my physical attributes.

"I have no idea what you look like. How will I recognize you in the restaurant," she asked.

I simply replied, "Don't worry, I'll recognize you."

"But you don't know what I look like!"

Well, I at least knew she was dark-skinned and curvy, so I said, "No, I don't, but I'm pretty sure I can work it out."

I could hear a little frustration in my future bride's voice as she said, "Well, at least tell me how tall you are."

"Why? Are you a height-ist (someone prejudiced about a person's height)?" I asked, laughing.

"No, I just want to know if I can wear my heels."

"How big are your heels?"

"Four inches."

"And how tall are you?" I asked.

"Five feet, nine inches," she replied.

Now even I, a guy of five feet eight inches, could work out that this would make her standing height add up to six feet and one inch.

"Sure, wear your heels," I said.

Once more, she pushed me to tell her what I looked like, and after much cajoling, I said that I would give her three options. I said that I was either: five foot four with red hair and freckles; or five foot eight with dark hair and blue eyes; or I was six feet, nine inches tall, weighing 750 pounds, with a hump on my back.

Now Renuka is a very bright lady, and she had worked out that she was not going to get a straight answer, so we ended the call confirming our date.

As we hung up, I knew exactly what she would do. She would call the friend who had set us up. I, however, had him on speed dial. I only spoke very briefly to him, saying that she was going to call and she'd want to know my height. "Don't tell her."

I was right, and he didn't.

That next evening, I arrived early for my blind date and sat with a clear view of the doorway. I wasn't sure why, but I was a little nervous. Suddenly, I glanced up and, right on time, I could see the woman I was certain was my date standing in the doorway. She stood there statuesquely in her four-inch, high-heeled boots and a long dress that showed off her fabulous curves.

As I walked over to her, I could see that she was holding up some kind of a sign. As I got closer, my face transformed into a huge smile as I read: *Looking for a man, 6'9" tall, 750 pounds with a hump on his back.*

And that, as they say, was the beginning of something beautiful!

THE POWER OF STORYTELLING

Bonding, Loyalty, and Meaning

As lovely and true as that story is, there is far more to it in the context of bonding. As I was saying earlier, every time a story is retold, it is an opportunity to re-bond the people in the story, and in truth, we have both told that story many times. However, the real power of the story came up around a year after we first told that story, during a communications workshop. We were out for dinner in a restaurant and we sat at the bar, chatting with a lady who was a complete stranger to us. After about ten or fifteen minutes, she suddenly says, "I know who you guys are!"

I could feel the wheels of my mind turning, trying to work out if this was someone we knew from somewhere else, but my internal search was coming up empty. So I said, "Really, how do you know us?"

"Oh, I've never, met you. I'm a friend of Linda XXX's and she told me how you guys met on this great blind date, and how you . . ." (looking directly at my wife) ". . . showed up in these super high heels and towered over him. It gave me hope that there really is someone for all of us, even if the picture doesn't quite fit what I imagine."

We all laughed together. It was a pretty cool moment, and as my wife and I sat down for dinner, there was a certain surge of love that came over us. The story was so powerful in the way we had told it that it had developed legs. It was now being retold by other people. It had become a story that inspired others.

The story of my wife and I meeting on a blind date had given that lady the meaning that there is someone for everyone, even if they don't fit the image we hold.

193

What Millennials Really Want

What does this have to do with leadership?

It has to do with your top talent. So before we get into "meaning," let's take a quick look at the group we are talking about and why you need to pay attention to them.

There's a good chance that many of your top talent are now or soon will be Millennials. As we said earlier, it's not that Millennials don't care about money. They do, but they really want "meaning."

By 2025, Millennials will become 75 per cent of the global work force. That means that the number of this generation who are stepping into management positions is growing every single day.

They are the largest, most diverse, most educated, and most electronically connected generation in the history of mankind, and any company that thinks they can ignore them should know it's only a matter of time before they will be out of business. Companies must pay attention to Millennials—in a big way!

What's more, if you are a leader in a large multinational organization, you will face additional challenges. Here's why: the research shows that Millennials are more likely to be attracted to working at small firms because they like the "start-up culture." They want to choose when and where they work. A start-up's culture usually facilitates them being able to dress casually, have workplace flexibility, and be innovative. Smaller companies also provide an environment where they can get involved with various business activities, too.

Millennials are generally not "one person, one job" kind of people. HR research shows that Millennials are turned off by the fact that large companies often have a disheartening interview process that makes them feel like a "thing' rather than a person with something to offer.

Just as previous generations were shaped by issues of the day (WWII, the Vietnam War, The Fall of the Iron Curtain, etc.), after the 2008 financial meltdown, there was an uprising, and that uprising had its roots in the Millennial generation.

Whatever you think of the Occupy Movement, its core issue was that of not trusting big business. What you need to know is that, even though it may appear that the Occupy Movement has faded into oblivion, the damage done to the willingness to trust in big business remains strong with Millennials. This mistrust rears its head all too often in corporate interviews, on social networking sites, and even on college message boards.

As stated earlier, many Millennials are not driven by money or success in quite the way Generation X or the Boomer generation were. This generation wants meaningful work. This means that they want to know what your organization stands for. Should they decide to join your company, they want to know if they will be part of what they see as damaging or improving society. Nearly three-fourths want to make a direct social and environmental impact. Millennials want to know that, if they join your business/organization, they will be able to make a positive difference in the world. They want to know what your company really stands for in action, as opposed to some theoretical blowing of smoke up the rear end of a new recruit.

*Employers must create a culture
that supports Millennials if they want to
compete against organizations
in their own industry and
the rising Millennial entrepreneurs.*

Meaningful Work

In recent research, Millennials identified meaningful work as one of the top things they want in a job. In fact, one Millennial's response was fairly typical: "If the work I am doing has no meaning or impact, I don't think I will stay with that employer ... I need meaningful work. I want to contribute to the company's strategic planning and be asked what I think ... A lot of Millennials find meaning in our personal volunteer experiences. If a company would provide opportunities to volunteer and give back to the community as well, we would be hooked. We just need to be asked."

As a leader, do you get that? I mean, are you really listening? Because that response just gave you a crystal clear vision of the vast majority of your future leaders.

That same research showed that, when asked what Millennials wanted from their job, the order was very different from previous generations. Only 12 percent said their priority was "promotional opportunity"; 19 percent said they wanted the ability to work from home; 22 percent said they wanted access to the Internet; and surprisingly, only 22 percent of those surveyed said they wanted a "good salary." However, 25 percent said they wanted "meaningful work." Simply put: Meaningful work is more important than salary!

By providing this meaningful work, you enhance the bond that will create the Fierce Loyalty we have been speaking about, and as I said earlier, such a bond means that if your competitors were to offer your top talent a "better deal," they would barely even consider it, because for them it not about the money.

So why is this? Well in truth, we could debate the social and economic climate and the impact it's had on this generation. However, the simplicity of it is, Millennials want to contribute. Millennials believe they genuinely have something of value to add. They want to share their ideas of how to make things better, not only in the workplace, but in the world.

As a leader looking to create a Fiercely Loyal team, you will need to listen to what is important to your Millennial Leaders. Pay attention. Find the common thread and connect everyone, particularly across the generation gap. Finding common shared values within your organization and allowing those shared values to drive your core business strategy will not only create a greater bond between team members, but also a bond in moving toward a meaningful outcome.

POINTS TO PONDER From Chapter 14 ...

- Full Monty storytelling allows us to see things we have never imagined and to feel things we never knew we could feel.

- Storytelling is the most powerful medium for moving the hearts, minds, feet, and the bank accounts of listeners in the direction the storyteller determines.

- Full Monty storytelling cements bonds, and bonds create loyalty.

- Millennials want meaning in their work, so you must create a culture that allows them to have meaningful work. By doing so, you enhance the bond that creates Fierce Loyalty.

Chapter Fifteen

Full Monty Storytelling

History proves that one of the most powerful ways to create meaning that will generate Fierce Loyalty is through storytelling. But why are we so attracted to stories?

The power of story has become an ever increasingly fascinating area of research, which is finding its rightful place in Leadership. Stories, as I am sure you've experienced, can move us from belly-hurting laughter to deep, sorrowful tears. Stories can change our opinions and behaviors, and most importantly, inspire and motivate us to take action we would never have dared to believe possible.

What's more, the latest scientific research shows that stories actually change the very structure of our brains; whether that is for the better or the worse depends on not only the story, but also how the story is told, who's telling it, and the place we are in (emotionally and mentally) when hearing it.

Key Elements to a Story

There are three key elements to an effective story. First, it must capture and hold our attention. (We've all had to suffer through a boring story.) Second, an effective story "transports" us into the characters' world. Third and possibly most important, the story must elicit within the listener a sense of seeing themselves in at least the primary character, otherwise known as generating a feeling of empathy.

As talked about earlier, stories do get remembered (my beloved and I meeting on a blind date). However, just because a story is remembered doesn't mean it will work in generating the kind of bond you are looking for with your team. All too often, great stories are remembered purely because they have entertainment value. Sadly, such stories are often without specific meaning. That's why you need to create Full Monty Stories.

A Full Monty Story

A Full Monty Story is a story that generates a directed, specific meaning in the listener that creates an emotional bond with that story and its meaning.

The difference between a "story" and a Full Monty Story is that with a Full Monty Story, you can feel the truth of it, and truth equals trust, and trust equals loyalty. When a regular story has faded away as merely entertainment, the Full Monty Story becomes even more deeply embedded into the psyche of the listener.

A Full Monty Story has far greater depth than a regular story. However, that depth doesn't always have to translate to length.

FULL MONTY STORYTELLING

It is possible to deliver a short Full Monty Story with powerful impact. As in other things, it really isn't the length that counts but what you do with it!

I guess you may be wondering why we call it a Full Monty Story. Did you see the funny and rather poignant movie The Full Monty? It's about six unemployed, and mostly out-of-shape, steel workers who are inspired by the Chippendale dancers to form a male striptease act. Initially, there is little to no interest in these guys or their show until, in an effort to drum up a crowd, they advertise that they will go "full Monty" and reveal it all.

Despite the movie's nudity, I am not suggesting that you reveal your Full Monty Story while being stripped naked, dancing to the Tom Jones version of "You Can Leave Your Hat On." What I do mean is that a Full Monty Story requires some form of Emotional Nudity, a willingness to reveal what would normally be hidden.

I do realize that this may be more than a little uncomfortable, particularly if you were brought up in the old school of leadership based on keeping everything hidden, especially from those you have considered your underlings. However, this willingness to open up and reveal is at the very heart of generating Fierce Loyalty, not only in your top players, but also in the people they lead. (Ultimately, this is how you want to do business, especially your marketing.) More specifically, your revelation must have the specific ingredient of being both personal and emotionally revealing!

Story vs. 'The Numbers Have to Make Sense'

Despite what you've been told about the importance of cold, hard facts, they do not and never will come close to grabbing and holding someone right where you want them the way a great story will.

We've all heard the advice from our accountants, investment strategists, and any number of other experts who say "the numbers have to make sense." Although that is a fair and certainly a reasonable line of thinking, it is often not what determines whether someone invests in what you are offering. The truth is, people pay what is officially "too much" all the time, and they do it willingly. Why? Because they "believe" even when the numbers don't make sense.

So yes, the numbers have to make sense, but unless you "feel right" about what's being offered, there's a very high chance that you will walk away from almost any opportunity that you don't emotionally hook into.

That's where story comes in! Stories can be a highly effective way not only to communicate but also to transmit important information and values from one person, organization, or community to another.

Stories that are personal and emotionally compelling actually engage more of the brain, and thus they are better remembered than simply stating a set of facts and statistics. In reality, telling stories—or, as it was known for millennia, the oral tradition—is the oldest known way to convey not only "facts" but also philosophies, values, and life lessons. Just as important, story is the most reliable way to not only have these things remembered, but also have their meaning deeply embedded into the teller, the listener, and in turn the re-teller.

Think about what this means. You must find your own personal Full Monty Story and be willing to share not only the glorious heroism of the story, but also the darkness, struggle, and possibly self-doubt you had to battle to be where you are today. That journey has given you a place from which you can lead with both head and heart in a soulful and meaningful way, which is precisely why you need to share it.

FULL MONTY LEADERSHIP TIP

A great story is about having the listener
see how they can become
the hero of their own story.

What Makes a Story Effective

You will no doubt remember a time when you heard what we are calling a Full Monty Story, because when you heard or saw it, it grabbed you and wouldn't let go. You found yourself thinking about it and or sharing it with others right away.

We get emotionally pulled into such a story because, if all the elements are there, there is a neurological response. Certain hormones fire off in our system, including the specific neuropolypeptide chain that triggers empathy. Once a story has held our attention long enough, we will likely begin to emotionally resonate with the story's characters. This can only happen when we can see a reflection of ourselves in that story. With such a story, even though we may not want to admit it aloud, we feel a sense of intuitive understanding that we, too, may have to deal with—or presently be facing dealing with—a similar difficult task or decision. As such, we feel the internal pressure triggered by what was an external story, and through this we may have to admit that we, too, need to learn how to develop our own deep resolve.

Both your brain and body have a powerful response to a well-delivered Full Monty Story. In the tense moments of the story, your heart rate and breathing will likely speed up, stress hormones will be released, and your focus becomes intense. All this is possible through the brain's brilliant system and the work of the mirror neurons that I spoke of earlier. This is why a Full Monty Story is such a fabulous catalyst for bonding and, in turn, generating Fierce Loyalty.

Stories bring us together.

Humans are Social Beings

Despite what we may tell ourselves on a bad day about not liking people, human beings are deeply social creatures. It's through emotional simulation that we gain the foundation for empathy. This is particularly powerful because it allows us rapidly to assess whether those around us are kind or mean, dangerous or safe, friends or foes.

Outside of those fairly cute and reasonably unusual YouTube videos of the cat and the parakeet being friends, human beings are somewhat unique in that we form relationships with a wider group of species than any other animal does. These wonderful neurological mechanisms not only keep us safe, but they also allow us to rapidly engage in both intimately personal relationships and the large-scale cooperation that allow us to work in leadership teams toward a common goal, building massive bridges that span great lengths, climbing mountains, and sending astronauts into space.

Don't take my word for it. Just think about it for a moment: everyone you now consider a friend started out as a stranger. It is knowing someone's story—where they came from and what they do—and discovering whom you might know in common that takes that person from the category of "stranger" and moves them into another category, even if it is just to "potential friend." It is only as we share deeper experiences (including past ones) in the form of stories that we decide to make someone a friend.

Earlier in the book, we identified oxytocin as the neurochemical responsible for empathy and bonding. Paul J. Zak, Ph.D., who is the author of *The Moral Molecule: How Trust Works*, and his research team pioneered the behavioral study of oxytocin; they have proven that when the brain synthesizes oxytocin, people are more trustworthy, generous, charitable, and compassionate. He dubbed oxytocin the "moral molecule."

His work and the ensuing work of many others show us that oxytocin makes us more sensitive to social cues. Depending on your upbringing, such cues can have an unfortunate side effect in that they may turn on the Rescuer in you. A Rescuer is someone who somehow always sees an opportunity to help (even when the person at hand doesn't want help). Sadly,

Rescuers end up doing more damage than good—but again, that's another book.

As pointed out, not all stories are created equal! Some have momentary entertainment value, while others (Full Monty Stories) transport us into the characters' world.

Many narrative theorists have the view that there is a universal story structure, and it turns out that the researched evidence supports that idea. These scholars claim every engaging story has a particular structure, called the dramatic arc, and that it is found in every successful play, movie, and novel. It starts with something new and surprising, and increases tension with difficulties that the characters must overcome, often because of some failure or crisis in their past. This then leads to a climax where the characters must look deeply inside themselves to overcome some form of looming crisis, and once this transformation occurs, the story resolves itself. Sound familiar? Yes, you got it; it's Campbell's Hero's Journey that we spoke about earlier.

What Are We Looking For?

Each of us can, given enough time, sit down and philosophize about the meaning of our lives. However, the bottom line is that we all are looking to be a little happier today than we were yesterday, and a little happier tomorrow than we were today.

Do you want the secret to happiness?

Well, it turns out that empathy is a key piece to discovering that illusive happiness. There is a cycle by which we must first engage with others emotionally. This, in turn, reveals that superficial relationships—even though they can be "fun"—will not bring us lasting happiness.

Here's what the research found: True emotional engagement leads to our demonstrating helping behaviors, and through that emotional connection and helping, we feel happier.

Just for a quick refresher: Story is possibly the most powerful way to move people in the direction you want (and to get the wrong people off your path as well). However, for the message to have genuine and lasting power, the listener (viewer) must feel empathy for you (or the lead character) by being able to see some aspect of themselves or someone who has been dear to them in this lead character. This is the beginning of the bond. In seeing this reflection, they must feel that they can, in some way, make a difference to the cause highlighted in the story (desire to help), because there is an unconscious driver at work: if the listener/viewer feels they have helped, they will in turn feel a greater level of happiness.

If You Don't FEEL It, We Can't HEAR It!

For your audience to feel pulled to and eventually bonded to you and your message, there is a need for you to supply something—something many are not likely to want to share—blood!

Relax! We are not talking about starting some kind of vampire cult. When I say blood, I am not talking about physical blood; I am talking about emotional blood. Here's why I say blood. Not too many folks will willing give of their own literal blood—every other week or so, we hear that the Red Cross has another blood shortage and is desperate for donations—unless one of their loved ones needs it. Then they will sit in the hospital for hours on end to give blood, and what's more, they will go out and evangelically get others to do the same.

The same is true with what I call "emotional blood." What that means is to give/reveal some emotional part of you that you would ordinarily hide and protect. However, just as literal blood gives literal life, emotional blood gives life to your story. It is this blood that will deeply bond your audience to you. This blood is universal and—surprise! Another name for it is vulnerability.

Your story must genuinely and vulnerably reveal you to your audience. When you willingly and genuinely give your audience a dose of your emotional blood, they will want to help because they will feel a bond with you, and as stated, they will go out and evangelically get others to do the same.

Earlier in this book, I wrote about Steve Jobs and his leadership style, and I stated that his style of leadership will no longer work, particularly with Millennials. However, Jobs' leadership was multi -faceted in that he was masterful at using what we are speaking about here. He knew how to reveal the blood that would bond.

I think most of us are familiar with Jobs' giving the Stanford commencement speech where he told the audience "not to settle." As I write this, that speech has received well in excess of twenty million views on YouTube. It was during that speech, in which he could have easily portrayed all his outstanding successes, that he shared being fired from his own company (Apple, Inc.) and how it had been initially a devastating experience. It was from the sharing of that bottomed-out experience that he was able to show each of us that we can still rise to the top, and that we shouldn't settle for anything less than what we love to do.

Rocky

Here's another one: Even if you don't remember any of the numerous sequels, you remember the Oscar-winning movie Rocky starring the then unknown actor and writer Sylvester Stallone. What you may not remember is that Rocky did NOT win the championship in that first movie. The character fought hard, in and out of the ring, and we got to see the fragility and the emotional vulnerability of Rocky Balboa. The character was able to fight his way into the hearts of tens of millions of viewers, many of whom, prior to seeing the movie Rocky, would never have watched a movie about boxing even if you'd have paid them.

Even though Rocky Balboa did not win, we lined up to see him come back again and again. Incidentally, if you want to understand the financial validity of showing vulnerability (giving your blood), you should know that the Rocky movie series has grossed more than one billion dollars at the worldwide box office, and that does not include the vast amount of money made through merchandising.

POINTS TO PONDER From Chapter 15 ...

- Stories actually change the structure of our brains.

- There are three key elements to an effective story. First, it must capture and hold our attention. Second, an effective story "transports" us into the characters' world. Third, the story must elicit within us a feeling of empathy.

- A Full Monty Story is a story that generates a directed, specific meaning in the listener that creates an emotional bond with that story and its meaning.

- Stories that are personal and emotionally compelling actually engage more of the brain, and thus are better remembered, than simply stating a set of facts and statistics.

- Your story must genuinely and vulnerably reveal you to your audience.

- Every engaging story has a particular structure, called the dramatic arc. That arc is Campbell's Hero's Journey.

Chapter Sixteen

Creating Your
Full Monty Story

You need to find the story that will lay you naked (show you as vulnerable) and thus allow your audience to bond with you. There are many elements to this process, which are an entire book on its own. However, I want to make sure that you have an understanding of the elements needed, so I will lay out each step for you to work on what will, in all likelihood, become one of the most powerful strategies you will ever come across for generating Fierce Loyalty.

Before we start, let me create an image in your mind. For the purpose of this exercise, I would like you to think of time as circular. At the top of that circle, at what would be twelve noon, is the "Present." At one o'clock, we have the "Transition to History." Two o'clock is "the Past," and between three and four o'clock is "Past Pain." Five o'clock is what we will call "Impetus," while, six o'clock is a transition from impetus to "Something Better." Seven, eight, and nine o'clock is where "the Battle" takes place. At ten and eleven o'clock, in our image, is "the Bridge." This Bridge leads us back to the "Present" or noon. (There is one further step I'll touch on a little later, but for now, just keep this circle in mind.)

Okay, are you ready?

I'm serious, because this is my secret formula for creating your Full Monty Story in a way that will bond your audience to you and, in turn, create Fierce Loyalty.

The Secret Formula

At "noon," you are standing in the Present. Here you start off by very *briefly* showing your credibility: who you are, what you've achieved, why you have the right to be in front of the audience. Then you immediately share something that the audience likely didn't know. It could be a devastating fact or statistic that is directly related to your message. This is what multiple-bestselling author Sam Horn calls her Eyebrow Test® and it's a very effective way of drawing your audience in within that first, crucial sixty seconds, as this is when the audience is making up their minds whether you're worth their valuable time.

It's called The Eyebrow Test® because what you share it, it should create a response in the audience that has them raise their eyebrows. Simply put, there must be some shock value in what you are sharing—but again, you must be able to show the significant relevance of your "eyebrow raiser" to both the subject you are speaking about and the audience you are speaking with.

Moving Around the Circle

Let me give you an example.

CREATING YOUR FULL MONTY STORY

One of our alumni from the Authentic Speaker Academy for Leadership is Karen Carter. She is a successful realtor from Vancouver, Canada. Karen understood that many successful single women look like they have it all together, but so often, they do not take the time to truly take care of their very basic needs. She understood this because her target market was, in fact, a beautiful refection of who she had been.

Karen decided that her focus (niche market) would be taking care of the real estate needs of these successful, busy, single professional women. She understood that what they needed was a place that they could call home, and that home would need to be a place where they could feel totally safe. What follows is the experience of seeing her speak...

Describing the Present:

The lights burned brightly on the stage, the music started to play, and the announcer called her name as the crowd rose to their feet with raucous applause. Karen, an attractive young woman with a bouncy pixie-bob haircut, confidently danced onto the stage wearing a form-fitting fuchsia dress. She briefly told the audience that she is an entrepreneur with fourteen years of experience, including eight as a residential realtor. Then casually asked how many of us had been in "coffee meetings" as part of our business. With agreement from the audience Karen pulled the entire audience into a scenario we have all experienced, giving us a sense of familiarity with her.

Then she flipped that familiarity into dynamic attention. By delivering a series of powerful eyebrow-raisers, including the fact that a woman is raped in Canada every seventeen minutes, the audience is left with mouths open, on the edge of their seats wanting to know more.

Remembering the Past

The next point, as you move around the circle, is the Transition to History. This is the point where you invite your audience to come back in time to a place in your history. Following that is the point where you will begin the setup of your Past Pain by painting a strong, visual movie for the audience to be pulled into. That, in turn, will lead to the vitally important place where you will vividly describe what it was like to be in that Past Pain. Here it is vital that you open up an emotional vein and spill the blood of authentic vulnerability. At this place in your Full Monty Story, your audience must be able to see themselves or someone they love in what you are sharing.

In her presentation, Karen took us back to a place in time when she was a playful tomboy who loved climbing trees and playing sports with her brothers. As she did this, we could all imagine either being around that age and playing that way or at least wishing we'd had that kind of childhood. She asked the audience, "Do you remember what you were like at thirteen?" Many nodded in agreement.

From there, she vividly shared the moment that ended her idyllic childhood in the blink of an eye. The audience went silent as she described the moment when her innocent childhood became an adolescence filled with rebellion and despair. The intensity was palpable, and we were hanging on her every word. She went on to tell us the impact of what had happened, how it changed her, and how she went from being a fun-loving tomboy in her favorite pink sweatshirt to becoming a multiply-pierced girl, dressed all in one color and one color only: black.

Once again we were completely drawn in; everyone in that room wanted to go out into the world and make sure that no girl would ever experience what Karen had. Within ten minutes, we had gone from an audience who was being entertained to an army ready to fight for her cause.

Relating a Personal Nightmare

Karen said her home became unsafe at age thirteen, when a step-sister moved in with her husband and baby. Karen loved babysitting. But one night, she was startled awake by an uninvited visitor – her new step-sister's husband. "I had that feeling in the pit of my stomach … that moment when you realize that something is about to go really, really wrong. And there's nothing you can do about it."

In a flash, her brother-in-law was on top of her, pinning her to the bed, his mouth and hands all over her, pulling at her night clothes. Her voice rising in rage, she vividly described wanting to scream and to vomit, but being unable to do either, because his mouth was on hers.

Karen told the audience that her childhood nightmare continued for another year and a half. "I didn't believe there was anyone I could turn to. I thought if I told anyone, they would blame me." And so, the rapes went on. She said she fantasized about suicide. Instead, she bought a gun.

Karen told the audience that she made the conscious choice between living and dying. She pointed her new gun at her brother-in-law and screamed, "It's over, it's done! You're not touching me again!" As she spoke, the entire audience went silent, and the tension in the air was palpable.

Then as only a master trained speaker can do, Karen flipped the mood of the entire room with a quick and somewhat menacing smile, recalling her reaction to the gun incident: "Damn, that felt good!" As the audience broke into applause, Karen said, "That was the beginning of my love affair with control."

She introduced us to the controlling alter-ego who had lived in her mind for so many years to keep her safe. This was an internal personality with the accent of a Russian spy and the sardonic name "Katya Ballzoff" (Cut-ya-balls-off).

The Impetus to Change

Next comes Impetus. This is the moment when the storyteller can no longer bear "it" (whatever it is that is causing the pain) any longer, and they realize they must do something else and they must do it now! (I call this the "Fcukit moment.")

Karen told us about what became the completely unconscious coping mechanisms she developed just to get through each day. She became a woman who felt she had to control every aspect of her life – and that meant living as a "lone wolf." "How many of you know a woman like that," she asked the audience. "A woman who can't ask for help, because she'd be admitting she was incapable of taking care of herself?" The enthralled audience was nodding again. Everyone knew someone who was "that woman."

In that moment, both women and men could relate; we all felt at least a twinge of recognition of ourselves because at some point in time, we, too, had created coping mechanisms around things that we couldn't deal with.

Karen shared with us that, after a year and a half of pretending and hiding her pain, there came a moment where she had to make the conscious choice between living and dying. It was like that moment in a movie that is so intense that, when the next thing happens, you want to cheer . . . and we did. At this point, she took that massive tension and flipped it on us, and the whole audience was suddenly in raucous laughter.

Life Becomes Something Better

The Impetus to change took place at fifteen, it lead Karen to take action. However, Karen's life shifting Impetus wouldn't arrive until she was in her thirties.

Karen told her audience that she knew that, in order to move forward in her business, in her relationships, in her life she would have to confront all the forms of false safety and let go of them—which, of course, meant confronting her favorite coping mechanism: control.

She had reached a new "Fcukit Moment"

A Battle in Three Parts

Life transitions into Something Better.

The next step is the transition from Impetus to Something Better.

The next steps in the delivery of your Full Monty Story are a three-part segment known as "the battle." The first of the three parts of the battle comes after having received your Impetus and moving through transition until you find yourself in that moment where everything feels/seems "much better." It could look like: finally someone gets me, someone actually understands, someone is here for me. It can feel like a place (literally or psychologically) that washes away so much of what you now see you've been carrying around for possibly years. Some describe it as the feeling of "home." This is the part we would all like to stay...It's just so much better.

The second segment of the Battle is when you feel the pull back of the old and the familiar. This is the point where, somehow, our ego-mind is able to whitewash the past. Here a person will likely decide it wasn't that bad. Because even though just a moment ago things seemed so much better, at this point, things start to seem "much worse." This is the point where we are likely to be filled with self doubt.

As an aside, it should be noted that this pull-back to the old and familiar usually happens because we have come to the realization that the problem we saw as solved in the "much better" part of the battle has actually revealed a far deeper problem that can no longer be ignored, and now things are becoming unpredictable. As such, there is a pull back to what, even though it may have sucked, was familiar and predictable. (In everyday life, this is where most people quit on themselves and on their purpose, mission, or dreams.) However, as Winston Churchill said, "If it feels like you are going through hell, keep going"—because the final part, part three, of the battle awaits.

The third part of the Battle is an awakening in that, as we keep going, things aren't getting better, but rather that things are quite simply "much different" than they were.

Karen's Battle

Here, Karen shared with us that she had been introduced to her mentor. She describes him as someone who seemed to look at her with mental-emotional x-ray vision, and although it initially made her uncomfortable, it felt so much better to know that it was safe for her to be seen by this person and that she could finally stop hiding. Suddenly, she had so many more options available to her, options she could not even see before, and life opened up, and everything was so much better.

We, as an audience, were delighted and excited for her. Once again, she had us laughing. I am certain that some members of the audience were wishing they were right where she was, at this point in her story.

The 'Much Worse' Stage

Karen told her audience that, once she began to feel "much better," she wanted everything to stop right there—but that's not how it works. This process of life, of growth, is not stagnant; it is moving, and as such, Karen entered the "much worse" stage of the Battle.

The pull back to her old, controlling ways came to her in the form of her inner voice, Katya. Katya didn't trust the mentor. Katya thought it might be easier to just "snip" him out of her life, to avoid the pain of change. Her mentor pushed her buttons and made her look at what she didn't want to look at. He made her face what she had not wanted to reveal to herself, let alone anyone else.

In the audience, we felt for her; we could relate. We, too, had things that we wanted to keep hidden, but Karen has shown us that this will not work. She made us laugh at her resistance so that we could laugh at our own—and, at least secretly, that was what we did.

The Final Part of the Battle

Karen entered the third and final part of her Battle in a vastly different state than when the Battle began. She told the audience how it felt to be supported by a team, where peers, coaches, and mentors had her back. She realized her life was now "totally different" because she was part of a community and no longer had to be the lone wolf. Her audience recognized that this was the kind of place they, too, wanted to be.

Now, Karen said, she has a voice. She feels it is safe for her to share her needs, her pain, her passion, her joy, and so much more, because things are totally different than she could have even imagined when she was living in her past pain. Now there is nothing left to hide from. In sharing her awakening, Karen has awakened within her audience the desire to have this kind of success for themselves and the people they love and care about.

The Bridge

The next stage of delivering your Full Monty Story is the Bridge. The Bridge is the place where you clarify the relevance of your pain story to the audience and how it ties into what you or your organization offer.

At this point, Karen shared with her audience that she knows firsthand the desire to control everything and the frustration of not being able to do so. She knows what it's like to hide part of ourselves because we don't feel safe. She pointed out that, as she has revealed here in her Full Monty Story, the experiences of her life have made her the kind of person who can effectively serve these professional women and their real estate needs.

"I can tell you why I am passionate about finding people a safe home," she said. "I know the feeling of being insecure."

Many people in the audience felt as if she had been talking directly to them. Each of us now saw at least a piece of ourselves in some aspect of her story. Those who had listened to her story understood that, in helping professional women find the houses "where the silence is more like a warm hug," Karen was also finding her own safe "home."

The Top of the Circle

This brought Karen back to the top of the circle and a return to the present. She had not only informed and entertained her audience, but she had earned their deep trust and now having been on this amazing roller-coaster journey they felt a genuine bond with her. Karen's audience now knew exactly who she was and where she had been, and they knew what she could offer.

"I am Karen Carter, and this is what I do," she said. "I will take the time to find out what makes you feel safe, what makes you feel secure, so that you can find your dream home."

As you can imagine, based on what I've shared with you about Karen's presentation, if you were in that audience and you were a single, professional female in the market for buying a home—or even knew someone who was—there is no way in the world you would be going elsewhere for your real estate needs, no matter how big or flashy another realtor's ad may have been.

At this point, you may well be thinking that this all sounds like it would be highly effective. However, when you present to the board, to the shareholders, the members, to your team, or whomever you get to present to, you just don't have the time it would take to deliver all that. I can certainly understand if that is your response.

But the Full Monty Story process is designed to grab your audience's attention right out of the gate, and in all likelihood, you and they will not even notice the time. Furthermore, you may be interested to know that Karen's entire presentation, from the dancing intro to the final words, was slightly more than eighteen minutes in length. She condensed her journey into eighteen minutes of speaking that converted an audience of strangers and skeptics into a group of supportive friends.

Deep Trust
While there are a few other steps to the formula, these are the steps that will help you deliver whatever your pitch is so that

it completely ties into the deep trust you have built during that first twelve to fourteen minutes of your Full Monty Story. Again, it's worth noting that the pitch steps are completed within seven minutes. All in all, the whole thing delivers a knockout punch in twenty minutes or less.

If you would like to see Karen's presentation, you can find it, with many other graduates' Full Monty presentations, on The Authentic Speaker Academy for Leadership site: www.ASALeadership.com

Why a Full Monty Story is SO Effective

Done correctly, your Full Monty Story is the most powerful and lasting way to generate Fierce Loyalty in a group setting. (However, the same process can be used one-on-one, too.)

Now, let me share the secret as to why this strategy is extraordinarily effective.

As much as we really like to think of ourselves as being wonderfully composed, rational beings who logically think things through, the fact is, that's not quite how we work. Human beings have fabulous frontal and prefrontal cortex brains that allow us to logically think and make those rational decisions, but the truth is, that's just one small part of how we work. Scientific research clearly shows that the subconscious mind is pervasive, powerful, and profoundly more influential over each and every part of our daily lives.

The subconscious mind is what's running not only your genetics and biology but, according to the leading scientists in the field, it's running more than 95 percent of your behavior. The challenge is that the primary programs that run our unconscious mind were installed in our formative years. This means they were not chosen logically or rationally, and as such, those programs are triggered by emotional responses rather than rational ones.

FULL MONTY LEADERSHIP TIP

If you really want to understand how the unconscious ego-mind is still running so much of our lives and what you can do to take back control, grab hold of another one of my books:
Don't Read This . . .Your Ego Won't Like It!
(It's available on Amazon.com)

The thinking mind is your conscious mind, while the subconscious mind is what houses the programs that run everything. This means that, as much as some of us like to think of ourselves as being strongly logical—even having a touch of the Mr. Spock—the truth is that any information you are using to make your decisions already has been filtered by the unconscious programs that are running in the background. Science shows us that the processing power of the unconscious mind is a million times more powerful than that of the conscious mind.

What does all this mean to you with regards to sharing your Full Monty Story? Quite simply, if you are going to have your people connect, bond, and be loyal to you and the organization, you are never going to succeed at doing so if you stick to being rational. We must engage the unconscious mind of the individual, and the way to do this is by triggering the emotions that are connected to the unconscious programs while giving the conscious mind the rational reasons to justify allowing those programs to run.

That's why, right out the gate, we calm the rational, logical, conscious mind by giving it what it needs in the form of credibility, while lubricating the gateway to the unconscious with what will preferably be a little self-deprecating humor. This is followed by the eyebrow raiser, which begins to open the gateway between the conscious and unconscious mind in that it's something logical (like a statistic) but at the same time it generates shock/surprise, which engages the emotions and the unconscious mind. As such, the conscious mind says, okay, you know your stuff; you are well read and/or researched. This gives the audience member a level of permission to stay engaged so that, when you invite them to come back in time with you, they will willingly follow you, because you grabbed their attention and they are now both emotionally and rationally engaged.

Creating a Movie

As you set up history to later reveal your Past Pain, you are creating a movie that will begin running in the audience's minds. A word of caution: You know as well as I do, some movies pull you in right away, while others can just as quickly lose you. Therefore, as you might have guessed, the set-up of your movie must have all the right details, while there must be nothing that is not needed. This is the part of the presentation that will require your inner editor. In deciding what needs to be added in and edited out, think about this: Does my audience care if it's day or night? Do they care if it's summer, winter, or any other season? Do they need to know how old I was at the time? You will have to sort out what's going to be relevant and whether it is going to engage.

As you move into the Past Pain part of your presentation—if you are indeed speaking to the right audience and delivering your message with full emotional vulnerability, not just in words but also in vocal tonality and gestures—this will trigger deep empathy in your audience members and their bond to you and your message will have already begun.

This will only happen if you give your listener an emotional experience that allows them to feel the struggle and pain of that experience. Remember, if you are not feeling it, neither will they.

Two-Movie Mind

It's at this point that the movie in their mind seems to magically split into two separate movies. There is the movie they are following with regard to your experience, but as that movie continues to run, due to the emotions generated by your story, there will be a second movie that begins to run side-by-side with yours. This second movie is something that relates to their personal experience.

Here's the most important part: The amount that you are open, authentic, and vulnerable with regard to your own past pain will directly and proportionately determine how vivid the now-dual movies become in your listener's mind. Once you trigger their memories, you are fully interacting with their unconscious mind and you need to be cognizant and highly respectful of that, because you are dealing with an extremely powerful process.

What makes this so special? Well, due to the way mirror neurons work (as we spoke of earlier in this book), the audience members' brains will now be firing in such a way that they will be feeling your pain and relating it to theirs, and as such, they will have a desire to help end your suffering.

The combination of the desire for the pain to stop and knowledge that they are impotent to do anything about it creates something extremely powerful: Tension!

The Importance of Tension
Despite what you might think, or how uncomfortable you are with it, know this: when it comes to delivering your Full Monty Story, tension is one of your best buddies! Nothing grabs an audience's attention better than the need to know what happens next.

As the tension builds, your audience wants you to break free, because there is something within them that also needs to break free. Then, when it feels like you (and they) will be crushed under the pressure of the tension, it breaks, and you catapult your audience out of the tension and into hope as you now show them that wonderful "fcuk it moment" of impetus. This is the moment of decision that makes you do something; when you do it, the immense tension is relieved. Your audience feels this relief, it becomes their own, and they are excited for you to find something better.

You won't let them down, because it's at this point that you begin that journey, the transition to the first part of the battle, that time where everything suddenly seems much better. Both you and your audience are now on a high. They see and feel not only that you've moved out of the pain, but that you seem to have found a safe place. Then, as in all great novels, plays, and movies, the roller coaster turns and suddenly there is another dip, and another round of massive tension is brought in. This time, it is the tension between expectation and uncertainty, and again there is the need to know what happens next.

That dip feels so intense and severe that you will, without doubt, feel the pull back to a past that, just minutes ago, you were praying to leave. Here you have revealed the second step of the battle, which is the pull to the past. At this point, your audience is most likely feeling the familiarity of their own pull back to their past. They may even have an ah-ha moment in the awareness that this was the point where they gave up and went back to the familiar rather than having the courage and commitment to keep going on to their dreams. Once again, we have generated a deep and palpable tension that we must allow our audience to feel so that they stay with us. You may be tempted to rush past this place in your story and ease that tension. DON'T DO IT!

Don't Rush

Here's why: this is the preliminary position for us to reveal that we have found a way not to go back, and that there is something else, something different than we or the audience could have imagined. This is when you step into the part of your presentation that reveals the "much different." This is the moment where you reveal a solution you are living, a solution your audience deeply desires, yet in all likelihood hasn't ever fully experienced because they were pulled back to the old familiar. They, for whatever reason, gave up and didn't keep going, and even though they are not going to put up their hands to admit it, they never experienced things becoming completely different. This psychologically triggers the desire for your solution.

At this point you, the storyteller, have shown that this is a heroic journey and that there is a way for them to traverse this dangerous terrain, because you have been there and can guide them. They are internally—and hopefully externally—cheering for you and your victory, because it has raised hope within them and they want whatever it is that you've got.

Now as you step across the bridge, they see not only the relevance, but the deep personal meaning to them of your having shared your past pain. As you step into the present, you represent something in them that they now desperately want to be; they are bonded to you and your journey because you engaged both their conscious and, more importantly, their unconscious mind. The clear contrast of who you were in your past pain versus who you are in your present, as someone who is living the solution they desire, is intoxicating.

It is at this point that your vulnerability has triggered sincere empathy, which has laid down a foundation of trust, and this trust becomes a road on which to call your audience to action (also known as your pitch).

Respect the Audience

It should be repeated that this is an extremely powerful process and you need to be respectful of your audience, because they are now in a vulnerable state. This is why, when my students move into the next stage, it is NOT a pitch in the traditional sense of the word. Here we deliver, in complete congruence with the Full Monty Story just delivered, what we call our ADC (authentic desired close). This means we only offer what our audience authentically desires, rather than trying to "sell" them something.

Here I must press a point that I am ferocious about in our trainings: "If you don't feel it, we won't hear it!" Please note that I am not speaking about hearing with our ears. No, I am talking about hearing you and your message with the heart. Simply put, your willingness to face and overcome your fear of vulnerability will directly determine your ability to become an Authentic Vulnerable Full Monty Leader who generates Fierce Loyalty.

That being said, whatever excuse your mind is running right now that somehow justifies you not stepping up to become an Authentic Vulnerable Full Monty Leader who is willing to show vulnerability, know this: IT'S A LIE!

Emotional Revelation Results in Trust

Audiences, even business audiences, will actually trust you more if you acknowledge your own frailty than they would ever trust someone pretending to be some kind of leadership god who can do no wrong.

When you reveal yourself emotionally, you quite naturally shine a light on a goal, challenge, or idea that your audience has likely been struggling with. This is the most powerful moment, the Holy Grail that was right in front of you yet you could not see it. You couldn't see it because, if you have been trained in traditional leadership, then you were trained to never go there.

So what is this Holy Grail moment? It's the moment when the audience stops seeing you on a pedestal but rather sees you as someone just like them, only with the kind of experience that they need. Think about it: if you are "all that and a bag of chips," it's easy for them to disengage because you are so different from them. But if they can see themselves in you and you did it, then it's possible for them to be able to do it too, with your guidance.

Look, I know the whole idea of delivering your story as a Full Monty Story in total emotional nakedness can be pretty scary, at least at first. But I promise you, it will be worth it. The payoff is far greater than you could imagine in that it generates such a strong emotional bond with your audience.

Here's what you will love: if you go out there and you fail at it, and at the same time admit that failure to your audience you will by the very nature of the process generate loyalty! That's the dichotomy: the more often you are willing to fail at this, the greater your level of success will be.

Whether we realize it or not, stories have always worked and will continue to work because they tap into the oldest part of our brains, igniting something within us that we may have locked away. However, a Full Monty story is a master key that can and will open your audience's hearts and minds, leaving them poised to spring into action. You now hold that master key. It's your choice as to whether you use it.

CREATING YOUR FULL MONTY STORY

POINTS TO PONDER From Chapter 16 ...

- ☼ The process of creating a Full Monty Story can be broken down into stages:
  - Present
  - Transition to History
  - The Past
  - Past Pain
  - Impetus
  - Something Better
  - The Battle
  - The Bridge
  - Back to Present

- ☼ Full Monty Stories are the most powerful and lasting way to generate Fierce Loyalty in a group setting.

- ☼ If you want to have your people connect, bond, and be loyal to you and the organization, you are never going to succeed if you stick to being rational.

- ☼ The more often you are willing to fail at Full Monty storytelling, the greater your level of success will be.

- ☼ A Full Monty Story is a master key that can and will open your audience's hearts and minds, leaving them poised to spring into action.

Chapter Seventeen

Fiercely Loyal!

At the beginning of this book I asked, "What does it take to be a successful leader in today's changing business landscape?"

I hope by now you realize that the single most vital part of successful leadership is creating FIERCE LOYALTY in those you work with.

But more than that, I hope you now understand what it takes to create that loyalty: VULNERABILITY.

In these pages, I've done my best to show you how the old model of leadership has changed and why being a CRO (Chief Relationship Officer) is much more important than being a CEO or CFO or any other kind of C-level leader.

I've tried to help you understand that to be a great leader, an Authentic Full Monty Leader, you must develop deep connections and bonds with those you work with and serve.

And I hope I've given you insights into what it takes to go on this "Hero's Journey" and why the best way to teach others to be authentic, empowered, and empowering leaders is by YOU demonstrating that model of leadership for them.

Some of the key points I would like you to remember and incorporate into life as you begin to become a Full Monty Leader:

* All notable leaders start out by being genuinely involved and concerned with the people they lead. It's when they stop being involved and concerned that their leadership fails.

* Loyalty is what keeps a leader at the head of the pack … not to mention alive.

* The work force is changing rapidly. The average worker stays at a job only 4.4 years.

* The money spent on training a new employee comes directly at the cost of keeping and developing current employees.

* Lack of loyalty and lack of engagement are two major problems faced by employers today.

* Forming bonds is an essential part of human nature.

* Reciprocity works because of our inner drive to bond.

* Monetary compensation alone does not create loyalty.

* People desire a sense of autonomy in the workplace.

* Providing opportunities for developing mastery is a key factor in keeping employees engaged.

* Purpose-driven companies are both creative and profitable.

* "Don't aim at success. The more you aim at it and make it a target, the more you are going to miss it. For success, like happiness, cannot be pursued; it must ensue, and it only does so as the unintended side effect of one's personal dedication to a cause greater than oneself..." ~ Viktor E. Frankl

* Money isn't THE answer to our problems. More money just creates different problems.

* Passion, curiosity, and joy are what get us truly motivated in life.

* Chief Relationship Officer is the most important officer in any company that wants to succeed in today's business world.

* People don't quit their jobs. They quit their bosses!

* To be a great leader you MUST become a master of dealing with conflict. Authentic, effective leaders must become masters of vulnerability and conflict resolution and they must help those they lead to develop those same skills.

* When your team does not feel safe expressing who they are and what they want, trust will fall apart. When your culture is not based on trust, ideas and innovation become repressed.

* A culture that generates Fierce Loyalty must give its people a sense of autonomy, ways to develop mastery, and meaningful work.

* Everyone on your team must know, understand, and be able to articulate the company's Mission Statement, Vision Statement, and Purpose Statement as well as show how these are demonstrated in day-to-day actions.

* Purpose matters more than profit.

* Purpose must be at the core of any company that endures, but to become a purpose-driven organization will entail growing pains.

* The real cost of doing business is becoming responsible and caring about your team, your customers, and everyone you come into contact with.

* The 4 C's: Cooperation, Collaboration, Contribution, and Community—are key to taking your organization to heights you've only dreamed about.

* If you want to attract and keep Fiercely Loyal employees, you need to do business from the standpoint of making a difference in the world.

* Leadership is service. You must learn how to serve from a place of compassion, caring, empathy, and vulnerability while holding fiercely healthy boundaries.

* Growth is inevitable. We either grow or we die, so leaders must challenge themselves to take in the information, knowledge, strategies, and feedback that will enable growth.

* A real "hero's journey" is undertaken to gain deep self-knowledge, meaningful contribution, and the real fulfillment that comes from creating a legacy.

* You must enter the hero/heroine's journey in order for your life to have the deep meaning you want it to have.

* Storytelling is the most powerful medium for moving the hearts, minds, feet, and the bank accounts of listeners in the direction the storyteller determines.

* Full Monty storytelling allows us to see things we have never imagined and to feel things we never knew we could feel. In addition, Full Monty storytelling cements bonds, and bonds create loyalty.

* FINALLY: Your Vulnerability is Your True Power and the key to developing FIERCE LOYALTY!

There's nothing I want more in the world than to transform it by creating AUTHENTIC VULNERABLE FULL MONTY LEADERS.

I hope you feel the same way.

About The Author

While free rock climbing in June 1990, Dõv Baron fell approximately 120 feet and landed on his face. The impact shattered most of the bone structure of his face, disintegrating some of his upper jaw and fracturing his lower jaw in four places. After nine reconstructive surgeries, no external evidence remains of the damage. However, this experience was life changing.

Before the fall, Dõv had spent years building a reputation as a dynamic speaker and teacher in the field of personal and professional development, but it wasn't until sometime after "the fall" that he began to see the beauty and elegance of what had really happened. The fall had become the powerful and painful impetus for the return to what he calls his Authentic Self.

Today, Dõv is the bestselling author of several books including Don't Read This...Unless You Want More Money!

Between 2010 and 2013, Dõv was the host and executive producer of the popular radio show "Full Monty Leadership Show." His radio show and podcasts have had over 1 million downloads, and his current podcast "Leadership and Loyalty Tips for Executives" is the #1 podcast for Fortune 500 Executives.

Dõv has been sharing his wisdom and expertise privately and on international stages with professional leaders for more than 25 years. He has interviewed and worked with leaders featured on Oprah, Ellen, CNN, Fox, MSNBC, CBS, Huffington Post, Larry King, New York Times, Washington Post, Forbes, the Wall Street Journal and many other top rated media. He also has a social media platform with over 200,000 followers via Facebook, Twitter, LinkedIn, Podomatic, iTunes etc.

In addition to being a speaker, author, and a radio host, Dov Baron is the leading authority on Authentic Leadership and creating a corporate culture that generates fierce loyalty, particularly when dealing with "Generation Y" aka Millennials. In that capacity, he serves as private mentor to top performance individuals, corporations, and organizations that are committed to generating both exponential growth and fierce loyalty.

Dōv's commitment is to take you by the hand and show you why tapping into your Authentic Self is the MOST important key to lasting and fulfilling wealth, influence, and affluence. His passion mixed with humor and "get to the point," no BS style are contagious. Within moments of meeting, you will feel a genuine connection with a man who authentically walks his talk.

Dōv believes that what the world needs today are more leaders who are Authentically committed to standing in their truth, sharing their inner genius, and empowering others to do the same.

He is currently available for media interviews.

To engage Dōv Baron to speak for your organization, leadership team, or to work privately with him as your mentor please contact admin@DovBaron.com or call +1-778-397-7717.

Made in the USA
San Bernardino, CA
25 January 2018